Piet van Schalkwyk
William Marshall

SOUTH AFRICAN AIR FORCE FIGHTER COLORS

Volume 1: East African Campaign 1940-1942

Model Centrum PROGRES

Warplane Color Gallery #2

South African Air Force

Fighter Colors

Volume 1: East African Campaign 1940-1942

Piet van Schalkwyk
William Marshall

Published by Model Centrum Progres, Poland
Warsaw, September 2018

ISBN 978-83-60672-30-3

Edited by **Wojciech J. Gawrych**
Cover layout, design and layout by
PROGRES Publishing House, Warsaw
DTP and prepress by **AIRES-GRAF, Warsaw**
Printed and bound in European Union by
Drukarnia O.W. READ ME, Olechowska 83, 92-403 Łódź, Poland

First Edition

Exclusive Distributor
Model Centrum
Warsaw, Poland
wjg-books@wp.pl

Contents

Acknowledgments

The idea for this book came from William Marshall. Little did we realise at the time, what a massive undertaking it would be. We aimed to produce a book that would be of interest to both historians and modellers, who would like to build models of the SAAF fighters used in the Campaign. We believe that we succeeded in putting together, what we hope, is an interesting volume, satisfying both parties as mentioned above. In this respect we have to acknowledge the great friendship and service that we received from the staff at the South African National Defence Force Archives and the staff at the South African Air Force Museum. Without their valuable inputs the book would not have been possible. We also received permission from a number of other people to use photographs in their collections, but need to make special mention of Tinus le Roux and Winston Brent, as well as the well-known historian and photographer Dave Becker, who has since sadly passed away. A number of the young pilots serving in this campaign continued onwards and served as Squadron Commanders and Wing Commanders in their own right later in the war. This is their story of how they started off with old equipment, but great skills and hearts full of passion. Our thanks to the publisher, Wojchiech J. Gawrych, for including this book in his series.

Introduction

The Hawker Hurricane Mk. I was the newest fighter that the SAAF could field in limited numbers for most of the East African Campaign. This aircraft carried the "Fighting Wasp" unit emblem of 3 Squadron on both sides of the cowlings. The rest of the force for most of the campaign consisted of Gloster Gauntlets, Gloster Gladiators and even older Hawker Furies.

In the early stages of World War Two, the Italian Forces in Abyssinia, East Africa, consisting of 200,000 troops and nearly 400 aircraft, constituted a grave threat to Kenya and the Sudan. To meet this threat three South African Air Force (SAAF) fighter squadrons were deployed to East Africa to counter the attacking Italian Air Force.

The three squadrons operated mostly old and antiquated bi-planes in the form of Hawker Furies, Gloster Gauntlets and Gloster Gladiators. Between then they did also operate a number of Hawker Hurricane Mk. Is, of which some still had fabric wing surfaces and two-bladed wooden propellers. These aircraft were also passed along between the various units, depending on the area that had the highest requirement. Among the three squadrons, 1 Squadron primarily used Gloster Gladiators, while 2 Squadron used Furies and Gladiators, with 3 Squadron being the primary user of the Hurricanes. 3 Squadron later converted to Curtiss Mohawks, but the fleet was almost immediately grounded due to engine problems. This plagued the type for most of its service in the SAAF. The squadron eventually ended up with a mix of Mohawks, again supplemented by Gladiators.

Unlike the Royal Air Force, the SAAF pilots all had to pass an Officers Course as well as their Pupil Pilots Course before serving on an active unit. There were thus quite an amount of Second Lieutenants and Lieutenants serving in the SAAF Fighter Squadrons in East Africa. These young pilots would make a name for themselves and many would rise in the ranks to high positions. A number of these young pilots serving in East Africa would within a few years be serving as Officers Commanding of the eventual ten active fighter squadrons that the SAAF had deployed in the East African Campaign, the Desert Campaign and in the Italian Campaign. Their slightly older Flight Commanders would serve as Officers Commanding Wings or as Sweep Leaders in these Wings.

The squadrons operated on all fronts in Somaliland and Abyssinia, and made a considerable contribution towards the victory that was achieved in that campaign. Commenting on their part, Sir Archibald Sinclair said: "When the Italian come to draw up a list of the factors that caused them to lose the East African Empire, they will place the South African Air Force somewhere near the top of the list".

1 Squadron

On 26 April 1926, No. 1 Flight was formally established in the SAAF. This unit was formally renamed on 30 April 1933 to No. 1 (Transvaal) Squadron. After various subtle changes in the name and equipment, the unit finally established at Waterkloof Air Station, equipped with Hawker Hartebeest aircraft. On 1 April 1939, the unit was again re-named to No. 1 Bomber Fighter Squadron, later changed to No. 1(F.B.) Squadron on 1 September 1939. On 1 December 1939, the squadron was again re-named to No. 11 Bomber Squadron, while at the same time, No. 6 Fighter Squadron at Wingfield in Cape Town was renumbered to No. 1(F) Squadron.

The squadron was finally reformed at Waterkloof Air Station during February 1940, under the command of Major N. G. Niblock-Stuart. The squadron initially had a strength of four Hurricanes and six Hawker Furies. The Hurricanes and Furies were crated and sent to Pretoria by rail from Cape Town and Durban. Here they were re-assembled and engines fitted which had been overhauled by the Aircraft and Artillery Depot at Robberts Heights. The squadron consisted of three flights with Capt S. van Schalkwyk, Lt B. J. L. Boyle and Lt S. V. B. Theron as the Flight-Commanders.

On 13 March 1940, 19 pilots and 24 ground crew left Waterkloof for Cairo, to collect Gloster Gladiators for the unit. They were flown up north in three ancient Vickers Valencia transport aircraft of 50 Squadron. The three Valencias completed the flight in nine days and on arrival the squadron was billeted in a camp in Abu Sueir, where they started their conversion training. On 1 May 1940, 1, 11 and 12 Squadrons were formed into No. 1 Bomber Brigade. On 22 and 24 May, the Hurricanes left Waterkloof Air Station for Nairobi, while the Furies were sent per ship from Durban on 26 May, arriving in Mombasa on 1 June 1940.

Training in Egypt started on 29 May 1940 with flights in a RAF Hardy. The aircraft was crashed on the next day while being flown by Lt Masson with 2/Lt Morris as pupil, fortunately none of them were injured. During June 1940, training continued at Abu Sueir on Gloster Gauntlets, with two Training Flights being formed for this. Two Gladiator and one Gauntlet Flights were also formed to stand by in case of an air raid or emergency. Familiarization tests and formation

Seven Hawker Furies were delivered in the Union during September 1936, numbered 200 to 206. They were delivered in silver doped surfaces, with polished Aluminium cowlings and were camouflaged locally before being shipped to East Africa.

Gloster Gladiator Mk. II, N5852, was operated by 1 Squadron in East Africa. During September 1940, the aircraft was often flown by 2/Lt John L. Hewitson. On 18 September he was engaged in combat over Kassala with two CR.42s and he claimed one destroyed, shared with 2/Lt John Coetzer, while Maj Schalk van Schalkwyk destroyed the other. On 4 October, Capt Brian J. L. "Piggy" Boyle flew the aircraft and claimed a CR.42 during an arial engagement over Metema, while his own aircraft was hit and damaged during the fight. He was in turn shot down, flying N5852, by a CR.42 on 6 November 1940. During this engagement he was scrambled from Heston to assist a lone Gladiator fighting against eight CR.42s. He arrived in the combat zone over Gallabat, just in time to observe his Commanding Officer, Maj Schalk van Schalkwyk, being shot down. The Major did managed to bale out of his burning aircraft, but his clothes were already on fire and he did not survive. Capt Boyle was also attacked immediately and wounded in his hands and legs. He kept on fighting back until the engine on N5852 seized and then carried out a crash-landing. He was then hospitalised at Wadi Seidna for a few weeks and was subsequently awarded the D.F.C. on 7 January 1941 for his gallant action by going single-handed into combat and to try and safe the Officer Commanding of his squadron. [SAAF Museum]

flights were carried out with dog-fighting also being practiced. On 2 July, 2/Lt Pare and 2/Lt Fritz both crashed during ground strafing exercises, with 2/Lt Pare being injured.

The first nine Gladiators left Egypt on 24 July for Nairobi. They operated as three flights being led by Maj Niblock-Stuart. On 29 July, Capt Boyle, 2/Lt de K. Viljoen and 2/Lt Duncan ferried three Gauntlets to Khartoum. These three pilots were back at Abu Sueir on 4 August. The second batch of nine Gladiators departed from Abu Sueir on 7 August 1940, arriving in Khartoum on 8 August 1940. The routing was from Abu Sueir via Assuit, Aswan, Wadi Halfa (night stop here), Station 10 and Albara to Khartoum. This unit was retained here for operations in Eritrea. It was divided into three flights, operating with one flight on "Standby" in the main hanger, one flight on "Ready" in the RAF Officers Mess and the last flight off duty. Two flights would be on duty from dawn to dusk and no night flying was allowed at the time.

This detachment was designated as C-Flight, No. 1 Fighter Squadron, later to be changed to 1 Fighter Squadron. The parent unit at Nairobi now changed its name to No. 2 Squadron, flying nine Hawker Furies, five Hurricanes and some Gladiators. Capt van Schalkwyk was promoted to Major and given command of No. 1 Squadron. At this stage the squadron consisted of 12 pilots, 12 mechanics and a few Gloster Gladiator aircraft. Operational conditions were very different as the squadron was under no Wing and thus the squadron's Officer Com-

Gloster Gladiator Mk. II, N5856, served with 1 Squadron. The aircraft was transferred to 2 Squadron for a short period and then returned to 1 Squadron in the first few days of December 1940. Lt Coetzer flew the Gladiator from Khartoum and joined the 1 Squadron Azaza Detachment, on 7 December 1940. On 13 January 1941, Lt Viljoen carried out a test flight on the Gladiator after a 30-hour inspection had been completed at Azaza. The aircraft then joined the 1 Squadron Detachment operating from Oxo, where Lt Young of A-Flight flew the aircraft. When 1 Squadron departed for Egypt, the Gladiator was transferred to No. 237 (Rhodesia) Squadron.

On arrival in Egypt, 1 Squadron used a number of Gauntlets for training at Abu Sueir in Egypt, while their Gladiators were being assembled. Three aircraft, 870, 871 and 872, would also serve operationally with 1 and 2 Squadrons until late in the East African Campaign. 2 Squadron operated them as late as April 1941.

manding (OC) decided what random patrols it would carry out. From time to time the A.O.C in Khartoum laid on some special tasks for the squadron.

One of the first operations carried out by the squadron was a fighter sweep over Kassala in August 1940. The main task of the squadron was the defense of Khartoum with a small detachment of two aircraft and two pilots sent to Atbara on 27 August 1940, to defend the local bridge and railway junction. First blood was drawn by the squadron in September, when Maj van Schalkwyk and Lt J. Coetzer each destroyed a CR.42 in air combat. On 30 September Capt Boyle took a detachment of eight aircraft to the aerodrome at Azaza. This airfield was about 10 miles (16 km) removed from Gedaref, where the RAF had based some Vickers Wellesley bombers. By mid-October the complete squadron had moved to Azaza, as part of plans to recapture the Sudanese town of Gallabat.

On 17 October 1940, the Italians struck with eight CR.42s and attacked the RAF aerodrome at Gallabat setting all the parked Wellesley bombers on fire. An enemy agent had cut the telephone line to Azaza and the SAAF contingent only knew about this when they saw the black smoke of the burning aircraft in the distance. The following day three aircraft scrambled without permission to avenge the raid. Guessing that the Italian aircraft had come from Barentu, they flew over the aerodrome and saw three CR.42s and some S.79s and a number of Ca.133s. They managed to burn-out all the

A Gloster Gladiator serving with 1 Squadron in East Africa, in the prescribed colour scheme for single-engine biplanes of the period. In the photograph the white and black painted lower wings can clearly be seen. This photograph also illustrates the difficult circumstances under which the units operated and often a lone sentry in a tall tree was the only early warning system that units had, to get some warning of approaching enemy aircraft inbound to their airfield. [SAAF Museum]

[This page] Gloster Gladiator, N5831, served with 1 Squadron B-Flight Detachment established at Oxo on 31 January 1941. On 3 February 1941, Lt Smith force landed at Azaza. The starboard tyre burst and the aircraft went over on its side crushing both port and starboard wings. Note the interesting white quartered wheel discs. [SAAF Museum]

CR.42s and severely damage the bombers. A case of champagne was sent to the squadron by the Army Commander Gen Lewis Heath, with his compliments. The squadron enjoyed the drinks from tin mugs.

A big battle was planned for 6 November, with the objectives as Gallabat and Matemma. The squadron moved to an advanced Landing Ground called "Heston", which was near Gallabat. Both Maj van Schalkwyk and Capt Boyle were shot down just before the battle. Maj van Schalkwyk died from his wounds and the A.O.C. flew down from Khartoum to personally take command of the squadron for the duration of the planned battle. On 8 November, Capt G. J. le Mesurier joined the squadron and took over temporary command until the new designated OC, Maj Laurie Wilmot, arrived. The unit was withdrawn to Khartoum to re-organize on 13 November due to the losses experienced in the period. They had only four remaining aircraft at the time and received additional Gladiators from 2 Squadron in the following weeks. After building up to nine aircraft, a detachment of four were again sent from Khartoum to Azaza on 22 November 1940.

On 25 November 1940, Lt W. H. Morris flying a Gladiator was killed in a flying accident when he hit the ground during a mock attack on a Hawker Hardy while based at Azaza. Gladiator N5851 was crashed on 14 December by Lt Jarvis, who survived uninjured. He camouflaged the machine to prevent further damage, until a salvage party could fetch it. During an attack on a CR.42, by Lt Gorden, flying N5789 on 27 December, the propeller was rendered unserviceable by returned enemy fire.

During December 1940, the squadron sent a Hawker Hurricane equipped detachment to Port Sudan. On 9 December Maj Wilmot arrived with Hurricane 285 at Port Sudan and on 16 December he damaged a S.79. Capt Driver accompanied him with Hurricane 274 and on the 16th, he damaged two S.79s flying Hurricane 285. The next day he damaged another S.79 with this aircraft. This Hurricane returned to Kassala on 25 January 1941 and was back with the Detachment on 9 March 1941. Capt Boyle arrived at the Detachment on 16 December with Hurricane 272 and left for Khartoum the next day. He was accompanied by Lt Duncan in Hurricane 273 and Maj Wilmot returned to Khartoum with this aircraft on 29 December. This Hurricane returned on 24 January, flown by Lt Coetzee and was damaged in a crash during landing by Lt Taylor on 5 March 1941.

On 12 January, Lt L. le C. Theron and Lt J. S. R. Warren sighted a S.79 while on patrol. The two Gladiators turned, climbed and carried out a stern attack on the bomber. After they had expended all their ammunition they broke off the engagement and while they were returning, one aircraft in a formation of three CR.42s, dived down and fired one short burst at Lt Warren. The CR.42 continued the dive and disappeared. Both Gladiators dived and levelled off at extreme low level. Two minutes later, Lt Warren's aircraft caught fire, crashed and burnt out completely. The pilot was killed in the crash.

On 17 January 1941 they moved to Oxo, a piece of desert on the banks of the river Atbara, some 15 miles West of Kassala. The pilots flew in five Gladiators from Khartoum, six Hurricanes from Khartoum and two Gladiators from Sarum. Patrols over the area and escort flights for Hardy and Wellesley aircraft were the primary tasks of the unit. Here the Squadron managed to claim five CR.42s, a Caproni Ca.133 and a S.79, as well as a number of enemy aircraft damaged. A number of aircraft were also destroyed in ground attacks on enemy airfields. With the arrival of 3 Squadron in East Africa during the last week of September 1940, the Gladiators of 2 Squadron were now withdrawn and sent to the Sudan to assist 1 Squadron, which had suffered losses in the attacks on Gallabat.

On 21 January the unit was again formed into three Flights with five pilots in each flight. On 25 January, Capt le Mesurier and Lt Duncan left for Khartoum in two Hurricane Mk. Is to bring back two Hurricane Mk. IIs. To ward against surprise enemy attacks, the pilots organised that one aircraft was always airborne patrolling over an advanced airfield, while the other were refuelling on the airfield. With the additional crew and aircraft which had arrived during the last few days the unit again re-organized into three Flights. While flying in formation with another Gladiator on 29 January, Lt K. A. Jarvis observed two CR.42s below and to their right. They dived down and attacked the Fiats. He fired several bursts at one and then broke off to engage another CR.42 which was diving at him. The enemy broke away and Lt Jarvis lost sight of him. Lt Smith, the other pilot in the formation, then confirmed that he had seen the first CR.42 on which Lt Jarvis had fired, crash into a ravine to the West of the Gura aerodrome during the engagement. On the same day, Capt Ken Driver, flying a Hurricane as escort to the ground strafing formation over Gura, shot down a S.79 that he encountered flying between Gura and Hai Khaga aerodromes. He again shot down another S.79 on 31 January 1941.

Hurricane Mk. I, 288, was operated by 1 Squadron during January 1941 at the Oxo Detachment. During February, it was flown at the Port Sudan Detachment by Lt Townsend-Smith. On the night of 22 February, the Hurricane was damaged by a Blenheim during a night-time landing, but was repaired and was still recorded serving with the Detachment on 3 March 1941.

On 2 February the squadron moved to Kassala, making use of the Agordat Advanced Landing Ground as their base. Five pilots, including Lt Smith, took off from Oxo the next day and routed via Blackdown and Pretoria Landing grounds for a strike against Gondar. South of Azozo, they found an airfield with five Ca.133s in the process of being bombed up on it. The bombers were immediately attacked and were completely burned out as the bombs exploded. At Azozo they found CR.42s taking off. Four pilots continued on a strafing run, while Lt Duncan chased one of the CR.42s towards the first airfield. Two more Fiats then attacked the Gladiators and Capt Boyle shot one down after a short combat. Lt Smith force landed back at Azaza airfield on the way back. The right hand tyre burst and the aircraft went over on to its side, crushing both left and right hand wings. Capt Boyle landed at Blackdown Landing ground with a flat tyre.

In the next week a number of offensive patrols were flown by both the Hurricane and Gladiator pilots and a number of bombers were destroyed on the ground. On 5 February, three CR.42s of a formation of six, were shot down in combat in an engagement between four Hurricanes and two Gladiators on an offensive patrol over Asmara. On 8 February during a standing patrol at Keren, the squadron again met five CR.42s and Capts Driver and Boyle each shot down one. During an offensive patrol near Asmara on 13 February, Lt Duncan, Maj Wilmot and Capt Boyle shot down two of four CR.42s that they met up with.

Capt Boyle was flying in a formation of three Hurricanes on 15 February on an offensive patrol over Gura. At about 500 ft (150 m) above ground level he saw three CR.42s taking off from the aerodrome. He attacked one, which immediately dived down into a valley. A dogfight ensued between them and the enemy finally crashed. As he dived down over the wreck, he observed the enemy pilot walking away, but limping very badly, from the wreck.

On the same day Capt Ken Driver, flying a Hurricane, attacked the leader of a formation of six CR.42s over Asmara Landing Ground. A dogfight ensued in which they made two head-on passes at each other. He eventually shot the Fiat down, which crash landed about 50 yards off the boundary of the Landing Ground. The Hurricane was hit by a single bullet in the left hand wing. On 21 February, six aircraft carried out a strafing raid on the aerodrome at Massawa. The Italians were ferrying in CR.42s with S.82s and assembling them there. Six Fiat CR.42s had already been assembled. The raid was successful and all six hangers with aircraft were burning after 1 Squadron had departed. During the raid light anti-aircraft fire was experienced and one pilot, Lt J. J. Coetzer, was lost, and his aircraft was seen to crash in flames due to being hit by the anti-aircraft fire.

A raid was also carried out on Makale aerodrome on 23 February. A Wellesley led the SAAF fighters piloted by Maj Wilmot, Capt Boyle and Lt Andrew Duncan with top cover supplied by Capt Ken Driver with three more aircraft. The Wellesley and top cover lost their way, fortunately the strafing aircraft found the Makale aerodrome. With radio problems the strafing aircraft could not contact their top cover and Maj Wilmot was shot down by a CR.42. Maj Wilmot attacked the left hand one of two CR.32s running up on the ground, while Lt Duncan attacked the other one. As he finished his run and was turning away, he noticed two fighters above the aerodrome at about 3000 ft (900 m). In the turn he then saw a third fighter diving down on Maj Wilmot, who was unaware of it as he made no attempt to escape. Lt Duncan cut across the airfield as fast as he could and fired a burst of tracer in front of the enemy aircraft. The CR.32 then broke off the attack and pulled up into a steep climbing turn and then dived into a steep gully to the south of the airfield. Lt Duncan followed him and fired at him from close range. After attempting a head-on attack, the pilot of the CR.32 decided to bale out of his aircraft, as his aircraft was already on fire. Capt Boyle saw it crash and burn out. When Lt Duncan looked again for Maj Wilmot he had disappeared. He and Capt Boyle made a careful search of the area on the way home but could find no trace of his aircraft. On this raid five S.79s and three CR.42s were burnt-out on the ground. Maj Wilmot was to remain a Prisoner of War until the end of the Eritrean Campaign.

Capt le Mesurier was again to act as Officer Commanding of the squadron, until Maj T. Ross Theron arrived a few days later to take over the Command.

The squadron still had a small Detachment at Port Sudan as well, guarding against aerial attacks on this important facility in the Red Sea. During the last few days of January and in February 1941, this was manned by Lts White, Coetzee and Townsend-Smith, all flying Hurricanes. Some RAF pilots did a bit of training in the Hurricanes, in order to assist with the stand-by duties should it be required. On 29 January, Lt White was booked off with influenza and he was relieved by F/O Chapman of the RAF, until Lt White resumed duty on 1 February. Two of the Hurricanes which served here at the time were 297 and 288. The last mentioned Hurricane was involved in an incident on 22 February. A landing Blenheim, returning from operations, took away the aerial mast and aerial and bent one of the propeller blades due to the flare path being laid directly in line with the Hurricane. The aircraft was again serviceable by 24 February.

During the last few days of February sufficient Hurricanes were received to re-equip the squadron and the Gladiators were passed on to 237 (Rhodesian) Squadron. The squadron in this period mainly flew reconnaissance patrols and strafing raids, under the direction of 203 Group. Road and rail transport were strafed on a daily basis, as well as any aircraft observed on enemy airfields. The assault on the mountain fortress of Keren began on 15 March 1941. This was one of the most difficult assaults during the East African Campaign. Once this assault was completed, the way was open to the final conquest of Eritrea. On 17 March, Maj Ross Theron developed coolant trouble while on a strafing attack. He force landed in flat, open country to the North West of Massala, in enemy territory. Capt Duncan landed with Maj Theron to render assistance. When the temperature had fallen sufficient, they both got airborne and flew the aircraft back to Agordat. The squadron lost one Hurricane shot up by CR.42s on 18 March, while Capt Driver managed to shoot down a CR.42 on 21 March. Another Italian pilot summarily jumped out of his Fiat when Lt Pare who was fighting him, moved into a good attacking position. On 31 March, Lt van der Merwe was lost when he crashed into a mountain in a crippled aircraft. This was the unit's last loss in East Africa and the next day, 1 April, Asmara surrendered, ending the campaign in Eritrea.

The squadron remained at Kassala until the final end of the Eritrean campaign on 5 April 1941. The final score for the campaign was 48 aircraft destroyed in air combat, one probably destroyed, 57 damaged and 53 destroyed on the ground. Their next move would be to Egypt.

[This page] Gloster Gladiator Mk. II, N5830, was damaged on 30 January 1941 in a forced landing at Sabderat. The pilot, Lt J. B. White, operating from the 1 Squadron Detachment at the Oxo LG, was safe. The Black lower surfaces of the left hand wings and the complete lower fuselage of the aircraft had been over-painted in a lighter colour as can be seen by the contrast of the under-wing machine gun pod which is still in Black paint. There is also no underwing roundel on the left lower wing surfaces. It appears that only the two right hand lower main wings is still in White paint. The new colour could be the SAAF Sky Blue, a light blue colour, which was used on other SAAF aircraft in the East African theatre.

2 Squadron

On 1 October 1940, when 1 Squadron C-Flight at Nairobi was renumbered to 2 Squadron, Hurricane Mk. I, 277/Q (ex-L1909), was one of a few Hurricanes that were transferred to 2 Squadron. A little more than a month later, on 7 November 1940, the Hurricane was again transferred from 2 Squadron to 3 Squadron, which had arrived at Nairobi in October 1940. Thereafter 2 Squadron primarily operated Hawker Furies, with a few Gloster Gladiators for some periods of time.

The history of 2 Squadron can be traced back to the forming of a second Provincial squadron at Air Station on 10 February 1934. The unit was called the Cape Squadron and intent at the time was for the unit to eventually move down to the Cape Province. The move never happened and the unit was on 1 December 1938 renamed to No. 2 (Transvaal) Squadron, after the squadron moved to the newly formed base at Waterkloof Air Station. The unit was originally equipped with Westland Wapitis, which was replaced with Hawker Hartbeeste with the move to Waterkloof.

On 1 April 1939 the name was again changed to No. 2 Fighter Bomber Squadron. With the looming war on the horizon, the next name change was to No. 12 Bomber Squadron on 1 December 1939, with 11 Bomber Squadron in Durban being re-named to No. 2 Fighter Squadron. It also received the grounded Furies of this unit, thus practically was unable to carry out operations. The unit then re-located from Durban to Waterkloof Air Station and started to train with Hartbees aircraft. With plans in place to move the 1 Squadron elements to Egypt for training and to Kenya for operations, the personnel of 2 Squadron were re-allocated to this unit.

On 13 May 1940, Maj N. G. Niblock-Stuart with 19 pilots and 24 ground-crew left Waterkloof Air Station for Cairo where they began training on Gloster Gauntlets at Abu Sueir, on 1 June 1940. Another group of pilots and crew under the leadership of Lt S. van Breda Theron received training on Hurricanes and Furies before leaving for Kenya on 22 May 1940, while a third group of personnel left Durban by boat on 26 May 1940 for Mombasa. These groups were all personnel of 1 Squadron, of which a section would within a few months be renamed back to 2 Squadron.

On 1 October 1940, while the Squadron was stationed in Nairobi, the elements of 1 Squadron based here were re-designated as 2 Squadron. The initial order was a verbal order from the Director General Air Services (DGAS), but this was soon confirmed by letter. The first Commanding Officer was Maj St Elmo Truter who became the first South African pilot to destroy an enemy aircraft during W.W. II. 2 Squadron thus took over the aircraft from 1 Squadron in

A Fairey Battle taxies out for another mission in the background as two of the Hawker Furies of 2 Squadron are seen on standby duties in the foreground of this photograph taken at Husseini airfield.

Nairobi and now operated nine Hawker Furies, five Hawker Hurricanes and a number of Gloster Gladiators.

South Africa purchased seven Furies in 1935. Six of these aircraft were put aboard the S.S. "Takliwa", still forming part of the 1 Squadron equipment. The five Furies received on 1 October 1940 were the remaining aircraft of these fighters. These Furies were equipped with the Kestrel VI engines and were thus the equivalent of the Fury Mk. II as operated by the RAF.

In August 1940, 1 Squadron received an additional six Furies from the depot at Eastleigh, Nairobi. These aircraft were Fury Mk. Is, still using 77 octane fuel and they were in quite a bad condition after their previous RAF service. These were followed by 16 more Fury Mk. Is during October 1940 and January 1941, this becoming the main type equipping 2 Squadron. The main role foreseen for the Furies would be to supplement 40 Squadron's Hartbeeste in army co-operation and ground attack duties, but they eventually carried out mostly defensive combat patrols.

2 Squadron's first aircraft crash happened on 5 October 1940, when Lt D. C. Uys hit the ground in a high speed stall with Fury 206, while doing a practise attack on a Hartbees near Wajir. This aircraft then burnt-out. Lt Uys was admitted to hospital with severe burns after being pulled out of the wreckage by a Sergeant of the Gold Coast Regiment. On 7 October Lt J. S. Wells left Nairobi for Wajir, in Fury K5669 to replace Lt Uys's aircraft. The two Furies at E-Detachment at Wajir now consisted of 203 and K5669. On 8 October the standby aircraft and camp were moved to N'Deges Nest, 25 miles (40 km) South East of Wajir. On 14 October Lts Wells and van Blerk carried out mock dogfights to investigate the performance of the two different models of Furies, with and without superchargers. Lt van Blerk in 203 was able to turn the tables if full throttle was used and a climbing turn, while in a normal steep turn K5669 performed better.

At dusk on 19 October, three Capronis, operating from Gobwen, attacked Garissa. The Furies of F-Detachment got airborne to challenge the attack. During the engagement Lt H. J. Burger, the Detachment Officer Commanding, flying Fury 200, managed to shoot one down. He was joined by Lt Wiese flying in K5670. They then lost the raiders in the darkness and carried out night landings on the airstrip.

During this period, the Squadron received two young Cheetah cubs from a local tribe and these formed the basis of its popular nickname in future of the "Flying Cheetahs". The cubs were named "Vickers" and "Spitfire". The squadron's first Gladiator accident happened on 23 October when Lt A. MacDonald crashed in Gladiator N5628 at Nanyuki. He was killed instantly and the aircraft burnt out.

With the arrival of 3 Squadron in East Africa on 24 October 1940, the Gladiators were withdrawn and sent to the Sudan, to assist 1 Squadron, which had suffered losses in an attack on Gallabat. On 30 October, the A-Detachment left Nairobi for Nanyuki where their new base was established. The Detachment was joined by the Headquarters Flight on 7 November.

Three Furies from 2 Squadron prepare for take-off at Husseini airfield, to the east of Garissa, in the South East of Kenya. These aircraft included both variants operated by 2 Squadron.

Four of the pilots from 2 Squadron photographed with one of the original Furies shipped to East Africa from the Union. The pilots are from left to right: Walter Stanford, Jack Meaker, J. A. Wiese and Lt P. K. Q. Rushmere. The pet dog was named "Winston". The photograph illustrates the type of airfields and conditions these pilots had to operate from and under.

The crew of E-Detachment at N'Deges Nest was replaced by B-Detachment on 28 October. During November this Detachment reported that it took them 20 minutes to climb to 20,000 ft (6,100 m) with the radiators not allowing a higher climb rate due to engine coolant boiling. They also had to land with flat tyres on a number of occasions due to thorns picked up during the take-off runs, fortunately with no damage. Furies 203 and K5669 were replaced by Gladiators N5672 and N5735 on 24 December.

An almost disastrous incident occurred on 31 October. The Furies of D-Detachment at Archer's Post took off to attack two twin-engine bombers overhead which were not following the specified recognition procedures for arrival. The three Furies was led by Capt Jack Meaker. In his first attacking pass he recognized the bombers as Ju 86s and broke of the attack. Lt D. D. Pannell followed him in for a firing pass and seeing him break off, accepted his attack complete and continued with his first firing pass. As he broke off, he recognised the roundels on the upper surfaces of the wings and realised what had happened. The passengers on board included General Jan Smuts the Prime Minister of South Africa, Sir Pierre van Ryneveld the Chief of General Staff, Major General Alan Cunningham in Command of the East African Forces and Major General Godwin-Austen in Command of the British Forces in Somaliland. Fortunately none of the passengers were hit in the firing pass.

On 1 November 1940, A-Detachment assumed duties at Archer's Post. On 9 November, with 3 Squadron now operational, the F-Detachment at Garissa handed over their duties to 3 Squadron and then returned to Nanyuki. On the same day, three of the Gladiators flown by Capts Masson (N5615), le Mesurier (N5651) and Lt Dimmock (N5613), under escort of a Lodestar, left 2 Squadron to join 1 Squadron, but Lt Dimmock, flying N5813, was lost at Juba when shot down by Sudanese village guards. He carried out a forced-landing on an island in the White Nile River. The second formation of four aircraft soon followed the first three on the way to the Sudan on 27 November, these being flown by Capts Kelly and Meaker and Lts Niblock-Stuart and Rushmere.

During December 1940, the 2 Squadron Headquarter was based at Nanyuki. Hurricanes V7382, P3254, R4103 and R4104 were recorded as serving with the unit at this period. The unit still operated attachments at Archer's Post Marsabat, Lokitang and N'Deges Nest. Between 5 and 9 December, the 2 Squadron crest of a

Gloster Gladiator, N5813, was shot down on 9 November 1940, by own anit-aircraft fire (Sudanese Guard gunners) and over-turned during the crash-landing on an island in the White Nile River, 16 km south of Juba, while transferring from 2 Squadron to 1 Squadron. The pilot, Lt. B. R. Dimmock, was lightly wounded in action. The other two aircraft in the formation of three Gladiators were N5815 and N5851.

Flying Cheetah was designed and approved and was printed on the unit's Christmas Cards for the first time. Fury 203 suffered damage to a wing during a landing accident on 8 December, but was repaired and returned to service. Four Hurricanes and eight pilots were dispatched to operate as Gayfly One to Gayfly Four at El Wak, near the British landing grounds, for the period 15 to 19 December. On 18 December Lt Gerneke, flying a Fury, was reported missing, after flying into cloud while escorting a Rapide with the General Officer Commanding onboard to N'Deges Nest. Searches on 19 and 20 December delivered no results, but on 21 December word was received that he had force landed 50 miles (80 km) North of Garissa due to a lack of fuel. He and the aircraft were both unharmed. The squadron suffered another loss on 24 December, when the 23-year old Lt John Douglas Niblock-Stuart of B-Detachment at Archer's Post was killed in a crash with Fury K5663. He was the younger brother of Major Niblock-Stuart, the Officer Commanding 1 Squadron on their deployment to East Africa.

On 29 December 1940, two pilots, F/Lt Blake and Lt J. A. Kok, were taken prisoner of war after both executed emergency landings. F/Lt Blake was flying Hurricane V7283 and Lt Kok Hurricane R4104, when they carried out forced landings during an attack on Savoia S.81 and Fiat CR.42s at Bardera airfield. The remaining members of the attacking formation were Capt Masson in Hurricane P3254 and Lt Colenbrander in Hurricane R4103. They observed three CR.42s getting airborne from a satellite airfield and going into a dogfight with the two Hurricanes, but they themselves had to return to base at Nanyuki due to being out of ammunition.

On 6 January 1941, the last three 2 Squadron Hurricanes, and their pilots, were sent to the Sudan to reinforce 1 Squadron. 2 Squadron now only had 12 Hawker Furies and three Gloster Gauntlets – 870, 871 and 872 – which had only recently arrived. One of these was in such a bad state that it was soon only used for spares to keep the other two airborne. The three aircraft did leave Nanyuki on 27 January for a new base at Buna, but returned again on 30 January. They were flown by Capt Masson and Lts Stanford and J. J. Wells during this period. On 11 January Lt Colenbrander and Lt J. D. Lawrie deployed to Marsabit with two Furies. Lt Colenbrander was promoted to Temporary Captain on 21 January and on the day flew a

Lt Adrian Colenbrander initially served with 1 Squadron, but was transferred to 2 Squadron when the unit was renamed on 1 October 1940. He would later serve as the Officer Commanding 2 Squadron in the Desert Campaign, and was KIA during 1942. He was flying the Gladiator in the rear background, N5851, on 20 September 1940, when it was lightly damaged during combat with a S.79. He was not injured during the encounter. The Gladiator was repaired again and was then transferred to 2 Squadron, only to be returned to 1 Squadron on 9 November 1940. It crashed on landing at Heston on 14 December 1940, while flown by Lt E. A. Jarvis, who was uninjured. He then camouflaged the aircraft until it could be salvaged, where after it was transferred to 6 Squadron RAF. On 26 September 1941, Sgt. R. Walter from 6 Squadron RAF claimed one S.81 while flying N5851. This was the last biplane claim by the RAF.

Gladiator Mk. II N5851 was one of the Gladiators being transferred back to 1 Squadron when Gladiator N5813 was shot down on 9 November 1940. This photograph was taken from the Lodestar that acted as lead aircraft for the Gladiators on the route.

Fury to Nanyuki to be modified. On 27 January, he and Lt Dimmock returned to Lokitaung, with two modified Furies, while the remaining aircraft at the C-Detachment was ferried to Nyeri by Lt Lawrie on the next day for modifications.

In addition to manning the base in Nanyuki, Kenya, a section of the Squadron under the command of Capt F. J. M. Meaker, was also detached to man a base at Archer's Post, flying Furies. On 15 February he was test flying Fury 213, when the front and rear spars of the lower wing broke outboard of the interplane struts. He managed to safely land the Fury, which was repaired with pieces of pipe, tin and boxes. After a successful test flight it was then ferried to Garissa on 16 February, where a new wing was fitted.

On 7 March 1941, the 12 Furies serving with 2 Squadron were deployed as follows: Furies 200, 203 and 215 were reported serving with A-Detachment at Kismayo, while 207, 208, 213 and 214 were with B-Detachment at Vittoria and 209, 210, 211, 212 and 216 were serving with C-Detachment at Mega. The Furies remained with 2 Squadron until April 1941 and were then transferred to 4 Squadron and 70 Operational Training Unit at Nakuru, Kenya, for training purposes. Their next significant service would be with 6 Squadron and 43 Squadron, back in South Africa. During the East African Campaign 2 Squadron claimed eight Italian aircraft (confirmed) shot down while many others were not confirmed and therefore not included. Only two squadron aircraft were lost in aerial combat with both pilots surviving but being captured. During April, the Officer Commanding and 16 pilots were recalled from Mega, Gigigga and Mogadishu and they left for Egypt by transport aircraft on 17 April 1941. The crew arrived in Egypt on 20 April 1941. It was intended that 1 and 2 Squadrons, would alternate in the Western Desert and in defence of the Nile Delta.

One of the Gloster Gauntlets operated by 2 Squadron during 1941. The Gauntlets were often used to escort the deHavilland Rapide used by the General Officer Commanding on his flights around the East African Theatre, as well as Lodestars used by other important visitors. They fortunately never met aerial opposition as the aircraft were not in a good state and would have had a hard time in such a case. The photograph shows Gauntlet 7832 before the aircraft was allocated the final SAAF serial number of 872. The worn condition of the Gauntlets can be seen in this photograph.

3 Squadron

3 Squadron was established at Waterkloof Air Station, Pretoria, on 9 September 1940, with Maj L. A. "Larry" Wilmot being appointed as the Officer Commanding on 17 September 1940. The unit was to be equipped with 15 Merlin-engined Hawker Hurricane Mk. Is, all ex-RAF aircraft, forming three Flights of four aircraft, with three aircraft in reserve. Nine of these fighters were being assembled at Wingfield at the time, with the remainder being assembled by No. 6 Aircraft Repair Depot at Eastleigh, near Nairobi. The squadron organisation continued smoothly during the month and the mechanics were being trained on the finer points of the maintenance of the Merlin engines by personnel from the Maintenance Command. Heavy rain in the area continued for days and it was feared that it could delay the arrival of the Hurricanes that were being fetched from the Cape Peninsula.

The nine Hurricanes arrived in Cape Town on the "Rochester Castle" on 12 September 1940. They were ferried by road to the Air Depot at Wingfield, where they were assembled. The first aircraft was reported to be ready for a test flight on 20 September. Once completed, the Hurricanes received the serial numbers 278 to 286.

The first eight Hurricanes of this batch departed for Waterkloof Air Station on 1 October 1940, while the departure of the ninth aircraft was delayed due to radiator problems. The Hurricanes routed to Beaufort West covering the 271 miles (436 km) in a time of 1 hour and 2 minutes. The next leg was to Kimberley, a distance of 280 miles (450 km), covered in 1 hour 7 minutes. On 2 October, the first eight Hurricanes led by Maj Wilmot arrived from Kimberly, where they had spent the night. This leg was flown in a time of 1 hour and 17 minutes. The ninth Hurricane arrived at Waterkloof on 6 October. The aircraft was flown by Capt Jack Frost who had reported for duty as a Flight Commander. By 8 October all ten newly appointed pilots had already undertaken some flying in the Hurricanes. Maj Wilmot tried out the machine guns while airborne on 12 October and the forward fuel tanks, which had been removed in order to make them leak-proof, were re-fitted.

After being advised that they would deploy to East Africa, the squadron was divided into a sea party and an air party, the latter travelling in Vickers Valentias and acting as a serving flight to the Hurricanes on the way up to East Africa.

Hurricane Mk. Is 289/A and 278. Note the Avro Anson in the background of the photograph. The non-standard A1 fuselage roundel applied to Hurricane 278 is visible on the photograph. Hurricane 289 became the personal aircraft of Capt Frost after the loss of 280, and his dramatic rescue on 15 March 1941.

A controller keeps a watchful eye on the Hawker Hurricane on approach for the landing during a training flight. Note the U-serial number of the modified truck, indicating the Union Defence Force ownership thereof.

The sea party left from Durban on 15 October 1940 aboard the ship "Durban Castle", and after an uneventful voyage disembarked at Mombasa eight days later, when they immediately entrained for the remainder of the journey to Nairobi. One of the Hurricanes was painted with the names "Suid-Wes-Afrika, South-West Africa" on 15 October, as funds for the purchase thereof were presented by the people of the Territory. The names were painted in the two languages on the two sides of the aircraft, just below the cockpit, the English title being on the left hand side of the aircraft.

The Hurricanes departed from Waterkloof Air Station on 16 October. The nine aircraft, led by Maj Wilmot, took off for Nairobi at 0945 hrs and the respective pilots and aircraft were; Maj L. A. Wilmot, 285; Capt J. Frost, 280; 2/Lt S. D. Marsh, 278; 2/Lt J. P. Upton, 279; 2/Lt W. J. A. White, 281; 2/Lt F. R. Glover, 282; Lt H. M. Torr, 283; 2/Lt R. H. C. Kershaw, 284 and 2/Lt J. Howitson, 286. The Hurricanes refuelled at Pietersburg and Bulawayo. Eight aircraft continued onwards to Salisbury, while 2/Lt Howitson remained behind due to a glycol leak. He arrived safely in Salisbury late on 20 October and all nine aircraft continued onwards to Broken Hill and Kanona. Due to strong head winds, only four aircraft proceeded to Mpika as it was uncertain whether the other would have enough fuel.

A Valentia was dispatched to Kanona with additional fuel and the last five aircraft continued onwards to Mpika. On 21 October, all nine aircraft departed for Mbeya in two flights. Due to bad weather the second flight turned back to Mpika and on landing there, 2/Lt Torr crashed. The undercarriage and propeller, as well as the air cooler, were damaged, and the pitot head and bracket were damaged. He was instructed to remain at Mpika until a crew arrived to repair the damage. The first flight had meanwhile arrived at Mbeya, refuelled and continued onwards to Dodoma. The remainder of the second flight then proceeded to Mbeya and onwards to Dodoma. The first flight had meanwhile proceeded to Moshi and then continued to Nairobi where they arrived late in the afternoon. The second flight, after spending the night at Dodoma, continued and arrived at Nairobi on the morning of 22 October, while the sea party and

Hawker Hurricane Mk. I, 280, later coded W, was the first personal aircraft flown by Capt Jack frost, the Flight Commander of 3 Squadron A-Flight. He would receive the D.F.C. for five aircraft destroyed in two days, of which four was shot down in a sortie on 3 February 1941, while flying this Hurricane. This was also the aircraft he flew on the day of his forced landing and dramatic rescue by Lt Bob Kershaw, who was to receive the D.S.O. for this action.

On 21 October, 2/Lt Torr crashed Hurricane 283 in a landing accident at Mpika, when he returned to the airfield due to bad weather en-route. The undercarriage, propeller and the air cooler were damaged, and the pitot head and bracket were damaged. Here the salvage team from No. 6 Aircraft Repair Depot, Eastleigh is at work with repairs to the Hurricane. It was flown to Nairobi on 13 November by Capt Theron.

the two Valentias with the remaining personnel arrived there the same day. A-Flight, under Capt Frost, was ordered on 24 October to assume duty at Nanyuki, falling under No. 1 Bomber Brigade for operations. While based at Nanyuki, the pilots carried out Flight Air Drill and practided attacks, with Capt Frost being recorded as flying Hurricane 280, which would become his personal aircraft for a while.

The next day, four additional Hurricanes were transferred to the squadron from No. 6 Aircraft Repair Depot at Eastleigh. These were Hurricanes 289 (ex-P3253), 290 (ex-V7281), 291 (ex-P3257) and 293 (ex-P3262). Like the nine aircraft received from Wingfield, these were all Mk. Is with metal wings and three-bladed propellers, versus the older Mk. Is with the fabric wings and two-bladed propellers initially deployed to East Africa by 1 Squadron. One of the Valentias left on the day with spares and a crew from Eastleigh to recover Hurricane 283 from Mpika. On 27 October, two more aircraft were transferred from the depot, namely 287 (ex-V7280) and 294 (ex-P3252). The unit had a sad day on the date however, when a while later, Hurricane 281 flown by Lt C. T. Gould was lost in a crash and the pilot was killed. The squadron now had a total of 14 Hurricane Mk. Is on strength, with No. 283 still stuck at Mpika undergoing repairs.

On the same date, C-Flight, under command of Capt S. V. Theron, was ordered to assume

Hawker Hurricane Mk. I, 284, 3 Squadron. The photograph was taken before application of the individual code letters and the unit insignia on 1 December 1940. The aircraft would be coded J and was the Hurricane flown by Lt Bob Kershaw in his dramatic rescue of Capt Jack Frost on 15 March 1941, for which he was awarded the D.S.O.

[Right & far right] The adoption of the new squadron crest on 1 December and the application thereof on the Hurricanes were clearly a big moment for the ground crews serving on 3 Squadron. A number of photographs exist where the members are posing for photographs next to the newly applied emblem on one of the aircraft. In the majority of these posed photographs, they are wearing full kit, including gas masks and their .303 Lee Enfield rifles, something which one would hardly ever see them with on normal duty days.

duty at Mombasa and they left for their new base at Port Reitz on the same day with five aircraft. They arrived from Nairobi on 28 October and at 1515 hrs the afternoon, carried out their first scamble, but did not make contact with the enemy aircraft. On 30 October, two Hurricanes from C-Flight, flown by Capt Theron and 2/Lt Townsend-Smith, left to form a new Detachment at Malindi, further North along the coast, from Mombasa. Two pilots from Nairobi replaced the two pilots at the Malindi Detachment and Capt Theron returned to the C-Flight Detachment at Mombasa on 4 November. He was replaced at Malindi by Lt D. R. Clyde-Morley.

The unit's Headquarters-Flight under command of Maj Wilmot and B-Flight under command of Capt N. C. Harvey meanwhile remained stationed in Nairobi. On 1 November 1940, B-Flight took over the standby duties at Nairobi. The remaining squadron personnel had since completed their training at Zwartkops Air Station and had meanwhile arrived at Durban, from where they left by ship on 4 November for Mombasa. On 7 November, Hurricanes 272 and 277 were transferred from 2 Squadron to 3 Squadron, for use as a reserve. These were the older version of the Mk. I with the fabric wings. The arrival of these two aircraft were followed by the arrival of No. 292, being ferried from No. 6 Aircraft Repair Depot at Eastleigh on 8 November and No. 295 (P8817) ferried across on 9 November 1940, thus leaving the unit with 17 aircraft on strength, as indicated by

Capt Jack Frost, the A-Flight Commander of 3 Squadron, standing on the wing of a Hurricane, with some ground crew members in attendance of the aircraft. Note the taped over gunports. This was always done as soon as the aircraft was armed in an effort to protect the machine guns from dust in the harsh operating environment. The ports were taped over in order to prevent stoppages. Also of note in this photograph is the fact that the camouflage paint on the cowling has been extended to a lower line than normal, in an effort to cover the sides of the tropical filter and make it less visible when viewed while airborne.

A 3 Squadron Hurricane Mk. I parked on a forward airfield. The crew have taken great care to camouflage the Hurricane in order to try and protect it from an aerial attack. The squadron's "Fighting Wasp" emblem is visible on the engine cowling, just below the exhausts and the gun ports have been doped over, indicating that the aircraft is most likely already armed and ready for another sortie, when required. Note the thorn tree branches placed around and on top of the wings for the camouflage of the aircraft.

the War Diarist as early as 23 October already. Hurricane 283 was also flown in from Mpika to Nairobi on 13 November by Capt Theron.

A-Flight at Nanyuki moved to a new base at Garissa on 8 November, while two more aircraft, V7279 and V7282, were transferred to A-Flight, but would remain in Nairobi for the time being. At Garissa, Capt Frost and Lt Allen and 2/Lt Howitson flew two scramble sorties on 10 November, but both proved to be false alarms. In one case the aircraft was sighted afterwards and identified as a Double Eagle. On a number of occasions in the month they would scramble, only to intercept own aircraft, such as Hartebeeste from 41 Squadron. The second sea party arrived at Mombasa on 11 November and left by troop train for Nairobi on the same evening. One of the Hurricanes allocated to C-Flight, 287 (V7280), was transferred to Nairobi on 17 November and it was replaced with V7282. On 17 November, Lt Clyde-Morley left for Nairobi in 289 to have the aircraft serviced. 2/Lt Howitson had a close escape on 22 November at Garissa. One wheel of Hurricane 279 jammed in the half-out position and the aircraft crashed during the landing, with damage to the propeller, undercarriage, radiator, wingtip and flaps. He was fortunately uninjured. The Hurricane was salvaged and removed to Eastleigh for repairs.

During the month a team from the squadron was dispatched to Bura, to prepare an airstrip and the tremendous task of cleaning away the bush and levelling the ground was carried out,

A 3 Squadron Hawker Hurricane Mk. I on standby at a forward airfield. The trolley accumulator used for the start of the Merlin engine is plugged in already. At the airfields where the unit spent some time, the crew soon started erecting shelters such as this one, in order to protect the Hurricanes. The roof appears to be from corrugated zinc plates, covered with two layers of sand bags.

Hurricane Mk. I, 285, the aircraft initially flown to Nairobi by Maj Wilmot, the Officer Commanding 3 Squadron, now has the squadron emblem and the individual code letter V applied to the aircraft. These two features date the photograph to post 1 December 1940, when the emblems were applied to the aircraft. Soon after arriving in Nairobi, the Hurricane was borrowed by 2 Squadron for a few days, and Lt D. H. "Doug" Loftus, with F/Lt R. S. Blake in the borrowed Hurricane Mk. I 286, used it to shoot down two of three Savoia S.81s on 25 October 1940.

amongst periods of heavy rain. Although the squadron flew its first operational sortie on 28 October 1940, it was not until 22 November that Lt Allen, flying from the new strip at Bura, drew first blood by destroying a Ca.133, killing five of the crew. 2/Lts Glover and Kershaw engaged the other two aircraft and although both were hit and damaged, they managed to escape using clouds as cover. Soon afterwards, the heavy rain caused the strip to be unuseable and the Hurricanes returned to Garissa.

The squadron's famous crest the "Fighting Wasp", with the motto "Semper Pugnans" translating to "Always Fighting", was adopted on 1 December 1940 and the emblem was also immediately applied to both sides of the nose on all the squadron's Hurricanes. Maj Niblock-Stuart, previously the Officer Commanding 1 Squadron, took over Command of the squadron on the same day.

Early in December 1940, the squadron was dispersed with the unit Headquarters and A-Flight stationed at Nairobi, while B- and C-Flights were based at Garissa and Mombasa respectively. The squadron received the news on 4 December, that one of the remaining Ca.133s damaged in the encounter on 22 November at Bura, had in fact forced landed in Somaliland on their way back to base. The crew were captured and taken prisoner while walking on their way back to their own lines. They arrived at the 3 Squadron base at Malindi on 5 December and all the pilots went out to meet them. One of the problems often experienced by the squadron, due to the operations in the wet and tropical environment, was that a number of members were frequently admitted to hospital, suffering from malaria.

On 10 December, four members, Maj Niblock-Stuart, Capt Harvey, Capt Frost and 2/Lt Marsh, took part in fighter operations over Kismayo. Although no enemy aircraft were sighted, heavy and fairly accurate anti-aircraft fire were reported by the pilots. On 12 December, the Detachment at Malindi, was ordered to move onwards to Lamu, where they arrived on 13 December and erected camp on the same day. As in other areas, the problem with mosquitoes was reported to be very bad in that region. An alarm system was installed at the base and during a test on 16 December, the aircraft used to test the system, was sighted 4.5 minutes after the lookout raised the alarm. One of the Hurricanes, 286, used in the test, was slightly damaged when Lt Allen struck a mound on landing. In the second half of December, B-Flight was split into two sections and Section II again proceeded to Bura in an attempt to continue operations from the strip previously prepared there. On arrival, improvements were made to the strip and previous camp and it was reported

Hawker Hurricane Mk. I, 280/W, was the aircraft flown by Capt Jack Frost on 2 and 3 February 1940. During these two days he destroyed one Ca.133 bomber on the ground at Afmadu and shot down another three Ca.133 bombers and one Fiat CR.42 the next day which were reported to be attacking own troops. Word was received on 19 February 1941 that he was awarded the D.F.C. medal for these results. He would in turn force land the same aircraft on the Dire Dawa satellite airfield a few days later, after being hit in the glycol system during an attack on the main airfield.

that considerable initiative was shown by various members in this effort.

Christmas Day was spent quietly at all bases and in Nairobi, the Station Commander and Station Adjutant visited the Sergeant's Mess, where they were joined by several officers. Thereafter, the Station Commander, the Adjutant and all officers present on the station, together with the Warrant Officers, Flight Sergeants and Sergeants, proceeded to the Airman's Mess, where they waited upon the Airmen for the Christmas Dinner. This was an old RAF custom which would be upheld by the SAAF squadrons throughout W.W. II. Very few operational flights were possible from Lamu and Garissa in the final week of 1940, due to unsettled weather with low clouds and rain showers.

After consultations between the Officer Commanding 3 Squadron and Maj Wilmot, the previous Officer Commanding, present at the Headquarters in Khartoum, three pilots and three Hurricanes from 3 Squadron, along with two pilots and their Hurricanes from 2 Squadron, were sent to join 1 Squadron, for operations in the Sudan. The Flight would be under command of Capt A. Masson of 2 Squadron. Capt N. C. Harvey, a Flight Commander from 3 Squadron, accompanied the Flight, being placed on special duty. Some 3 Squadron maintenance personnel accompanied the Flight in a Junkers Ju 52. Capt Harvey and the personnel returned to Nairobi on 11 January, with their duties completed.

During January 1941, Capt Frost took part in trials with the new radar system that was designed and built in South Africa and which had now been dispatched and erected in the Nairobi area. At Bura, the crew had now begun to build shelters for their Hurricanes and good progress was reported on 11 January. On 14 January it was reported that the repainting of the aircraft at Mombasa was continuing. This was an effort to combat the effect that the harsh climate had on the airframes and prolong their serviceability. Various interceptions during the remainder of January were carried out, and a number proved to be own aircraft, such as Hartebeeste and Martin Marylands. On 22 January, the pilots at Lamu took off to investigate an unidentified aircraft, but the target disappeared into the clouds and they failed to intercept it. It was later reported to be an enemy aircraft dropping pamphlets over a wide area from Witu to Mkonumbi. On 29 January, Capt Frost and Lt Dudley took off from Garissa to Nanyuki, after having been appointed escorts for General Wavell, General Officer Commanding, Middle East. They proceeded from the base at Nanyuki to Marsabat and Dukana, returning to Nanyuki in the afternoon, where they spent the night. On the last day of the month, Capt Frost, who had proceeded in a Hartebeest to Ali Gabe, to inspect the field

The burnt out wreck of Hurricane Mk. I, 287, flown by Capt Theron from Jiggiga on 29 March. He had to carry out a forced landing due to being hit in the glycol system and the wreck was set alight by the attacking CR.42s.

Hawker Hurricane Mk. I, 286/K, 3 Squadron. This Hurricane was delivered to the squadron from Wingfield a few days later than the original eight aircraft due to a radiator problem. On the flight to Nairobi, flown by 2/Lt J. Howitson, the Hurricane again had problems with a glycol leak. The Hurricane served with B-Flight Section 1, while deployed at Garissa and Margherita during February 1941. It was often flown by Lt Palfrey during this period.

The armourers are working on the underwing machine guns of this 3 Squadron Gladiator. The gun fairings have been removed and are lying between the undercarriage wheels. This Gladiator also has the non-standard camouflage pattern seen on the rudder of a number of the ex-94 Squadron aircraft and the narrow bands in the tail fin flash. The non-standard fuselage roundel with the big white circle and no Yellow outer circle has also been seen on at least one more of these Gladiators.

for a possible deployment there, reported back that he was attacked by two CR.42s as he was preparing for take-off at Ali Gabe. While on the ground, one Fiat dived and opened fire, but only one hit in the fin was registered. After getting airborne, Capt Frost kept low over the trees until he had sufficient speed to allow him to return the attack. The two Fiats however, at this stage, broke away in a climbing turn into the sun and were lost in the clouds.

The beginning of February saw the squadron units on the move again and B-Flight Section II had moved to Galma Galla on 1 February with A-Flight Section I moving to Ali Gabe. Capt Theron had a narrow escape during this period. He was flying to Ali Gabe to deliver some urgently needed tyres and tubes, when soon after passing Garissa, he realised that he would not arrive there before darkness set in. He returned and landed at Garissa after two attempts. At the first attempt, just before touch down, he saw a Puss Moth in his landing lights ahead of him and did a steep climbing turn in an attempt to miss the aircraft. He actually touched the ground with his left wing tip during this manoeuver. On his second attempt, with the aid of vehicle lights, he carried out a perfect landing. The squadron also received word during this period to prepare for a possible move of the Headquarters to Garissa and the Officer Commanding went there on 2 February to inspect possible sites for such a move.

After failing to find any enemy aircraft after a scramble from Ali Gabe on the day, Capt Frost and Lt Howitson continued to Afmadu and approached the airfield from the South. They saw a Ca.133 on the airfield and Capt Frost immediately attacked it. After a couple of bursts from his guns, the aircraft caught fire and was completely burned out. Lt Marsh took off on the third warning of aircraft early in the morning of 3 February and intercepted five CR.42s over Afmadu in close formation. He immediately attacked the number four of the formation. The enemy half-rolled and dived away, escaping in clouds. The remainder had by then also all escaped into the available cloud cover. At 0945 hrs on the same morning, Capt Frost encountered three Ca.133 engaged in bombing the Division. He immediately attacked the first aircraft head-on. At the same time, two CR.42s appeared on the scene and attacked him, one head-on and the other from astern. He fired on the head-on aircraft and then broke away in a diving turn, again continuing the attack on the Ca.133s. Two of the three aircraft immediately glided down and by then he was again attacked by the two fighters, following their same tactic as before. The one fighter, however, broke off too early and Capt Frost immediately shot it down. He immediately continued his attack on the last Ca.133 and shot this aircraft down as well, thus shooting down four enemy aircraft in one engagement. He had thus now bagged five enemy aircraft, all confirmed by other sources and on 19 February he was granted the immediate award of the D.F.C. for this feat.

During an operation from Galma Galla on the same morning, Capt Theron and Lts Dudley and Upton took off for Gobwen, where they were to escort attacking Ju 86 bombers. The three Hurricanes arrived over the target five minutes before the bombers and by the time they arrived overhead, Capt Theron had already set fire to

Gloster Gladiator Mk. II, N2289/GO-A, operated by 3 Squadron during the East African Campaign. The unit received nine Gladiators from 94 Squadron on the 18 April 1941 and this aircraft still carries the GO squadron code of this unit. It also has a tail band around the rear fuselage, in what is believed to be standard RAF Sky. The Gladiators received from 94 Squadron were all numbered in the N22xx series, indicating that they had been built by the Gloster Aircraft Co. Ltd. during 1938.

two CR.42s on the satellite airfield, with Lt Upton keeping an eye open overhead for possible fighter interference and Lt Dudley attacking the main airfield at Gobwen, setting one Ca.133 on fire. As the bombers approached, Lt Upton dived down on the Gobwen airfield to indicate the targets to the Ju 86 bombers and he set fire to a Ca.133 during this attacking pass.

On 4 February, B-Flight Section II at Galma Galla received orders to move forward to Kolbio and this was carried out on the same day. At Kolbio, the crews selected positions for the parking of aircraft during standby periods while different positions were chosen for the parking of the Hurricanes during night time. By now, between 5 and 9 February 1941, the Headquarters elements were also busy with their preparations for the intended move to Garissa, with the convoy moving out on 9 February. Messages of congratulations on the good results achieved in the previous few days were received from General Cunningham, General Officer Commanding East African Forces and Air Commodore Sowry, Air Officer Commanding, East Africa. The A-Flight Hurricanes under Capt Frost from the Ali Gabe Section also moved forward to Beles Gugani on 9 February, with the equipment and remaining personnel arriving late in the afternoon, setting up a temporary camp for the night.

Afmadu fell on 11 February and Brigadier Daniel, who had just returned from there to Beles Gugani, ordered A-Flight to immediately move forward and re-deploy there. The aircraft left immediately and the ground support arrived there just after darkness had fell. Although enemy bombers flew overhead during the night, their bombs were dropped several miles away.

On 12 February the airfield was again attacked during the night and some bombs fell as close as within 50 yards from the Hurricanes when one stick of heavy bombs were dropped. Fortunately no damage was done to any aircraft and no persons were injured. This was the first experience that the men had of being on the receiving end of enemy bombs. During a second attack later at night, a bomber flying very low was met with severe and accurate anti-aircraft return fire and was shot down after dropping his bombs some distance away. Four of the crew were killed and the pilot was seriously wounded. On the night of 13 February, the aircraft was moved back to Beles Gugani for the evening as precaution against further bombing attacks. Lt Marsh struck a hole on landing, causing the undercarriage to give way and damaging the aircraft.

This was a period of good results for the attacking ground forces, but it also left the squad-

Hawker Hurricane Mk. I, M, 3 Squadron at Mogadiscio during March 1941. The author has not been able to trace any sequence or pattern for the code letters from the available photographs of the squadron's aircraft and the serial number is not discernable from the photograph. The code letter appears to be in a Light Grey colour, as the dark outer ring of the roundel and dark forward band of the fin flash, which were Yellow and Orange respectively indicate the use of an orthochromatic film.

ron sections in a very fluid state and a number of moves were undertaken shortly on top of each other. The Afmadu Detachment was also part of this experience and they had to move again on 15 February, this time to Gobwen satellite airfield, an airfield which they had attacked with good results, just 12 days earlier. No one complained though, as the strip at Afmadu was in a poor condition and the crews had to regularly fix punctures due to the amount of thorns and stones present. Lt Glover from A-Flight attacked two Savoia S.79s on 15 February, of which the one was seen to trail black smoke after three attacks and the other managed to escape in cloud cover. The Headquarters Flight was also not spared from the moving around and they departed to Kismayo, operating from there by 16 February. This airfield was shared with some of the bombers and Army co-operation squadrons and were becoming quite busy during this period. Hurricane 286 was also reported to be serviceable again with B-Flight after its previous landing incident and was operating from Garissa on 17 February. On the same day, the B-Flight Section II Detachment at Kolbio, was also ordered to proceed to Kismayo, adding to the amount of aircraft already there. To give an impression of what these moves meant to the ground staff, it needs to be mentioned that it on average took them four hours every time to move as little as 29 miles (52 km) due to the poor condition of the roads. On 25 February, Capt Harvey and Lt Palfrey, the last members of B-Flight at Garissa, left in Hurricanes 294 and 286 and also re-deployed to Kismayo. On arrival there, B-Flight Section I was ordered to take up standby duties from Margherita, and Lts Venter and Palfrey continued onwards to their new position. The next day B-Flight Section II started off from Kismayo for operations over Mogadiscio, only to discover that the infantry had already occupied it the day before. Their move thus carried on and by afternoon B-Flight Section II had re-deployed to Mogadiscio. The Headquarters soon followed the Flights to this new base. This airfield had hangers available and here for the first time in a long period, maintenance could be carried out under some descent cover. The crew commenced with a 120-hour inspection, the first to be carried out on one of their Hurricanes.

The next two months saw the unit advancing on Addis via Gorrahai, Dagah Bur, Jiggiga and Dire Dawa. By middle-March the Headquarters and A-Flight were also already deployed at Dagah Bur. During all these moves, C-Flight remained deployed at Port Reitz, for the defence of the Mombasa area. Capt Theron and Lt Venter were inbound to Dagah Bur on 13 March and arrived as two CR.42s were attacking the field.

[This page] Hawker Hurricane Mk. I, 290/B (ex-V7281), of 3 Squadron in East Africa. These photographs show the Hurricane in three different eras of its career with 3 Squadron. In the top photograph the aircraft is seen sharing a forward airfield with a Ju 52 transport aircraft that was used on the shuttle service between the Union and East Africa. It is camouflaged in a typical A-scheme pattern and has standard markings, the squadron emblem and individual code letter applied. Bottom right, a patched 290 from the combat on 29 March, is undergoing maintenance at Addis Ababa in April 1941. Bottom, the wrecked remains of the Hurricane can be seen after it was crash landed at Addis Ababa on 24 May 1941 by Lt A. S. Venter. An isolated truck which had most likely been booby trapped blew up in his face during a strafing pass on the vehicle and he managed to crash land the stricken Hurricane at base. An order was immediately issued forbidding attacks on such isolated vehicles after this incident.

Gloster Gladiator Mk. II, GO-B, operated by 3 Squadron during the East African Campaign. It also has a tail band around the rear fuselage, in what is believed to be standard RAF Sky. Note the modified fin flash with the narrow White band. The two pilots from 3 Squadron are Lts G. R. Jacobs (left) and Basil Dold. Lt Jacobs was killed in a Mohawk accident during November 1941, while Lt Dold was posted to 1 Squadron in Egypt in August 1941. Note the replacement canopy still in Aluminium finish.

Lt Dudley, who was just taking off to defend the base, was attacked by the Fiats and shot down immediately. He was killed by the machine gun fire and was thrown clear of the burning wreck as it crashed. At this time the other two Hurricanes arrived on the scene and they managed to shoot down both the attacking fighters.

On 15 March during an attack on the Dire Dawa airfield complex, the following were claimed by the 3 Squadron pilots (including all three Flight Commanders) partaking in this operation; four bombers and one fighter burned on the main airfield and six fighters burned or damaged on the satellite strip, with a further three fighters shot down during aerial combat in the area.

The attack was repeated in the afternoon and this time it was unfortunately not with such good results. Capt Harvey was shot down by ant-aircraft fire during an attacking pass and his aircraft was seen to burst into flames and crash. Another disaster of great magnitude was prevented by the gallant action of Lt R. H. C. "Bob" Kershaw. During the attack on the main airfield, Capt Frost's Hurricane was hit in the Glycol system and he carried out a successful forced landing on the satellite airfield. He exited his stricken Hurricane and immediately set fire to it, using his Very pistol. Lt Kershaw, observing this, landed his Hurricane under enemy fire on the strip and taxied up to his Flight Commander. Capt Frost jumped aboard, sat on his lap and together they successfully flew the Hurricane back to Dagahbur, with Capt Frost flying and Lt Kershaw operating the landing gear and flaps. Lt Kershaw received the D.S.O. for his courage, determination and devotion to duty in this gallant action in the face of enemy fire. The total enemy losses between the two sorties on the day was 18 bombers shot down, burnt or destroyed and 11 fighters shot down, burnt or damaged.

Capt S. van B. Theron, another officer that would be awarded the D.F.C. on 22 March, also shot down a CR.32 on 20 March while escorting bombers over Dire Dawa and Harrar. During the second last week of the month, the Headquarters Flight moved off to Jiggiga. Here the Hurricanes on standby were skillfully camouflaged among trees at the end of the runway. On 24 March Capt Frost and Lt Howitson attacked Dire Dawa and managed to set a number of enemy bombers alight.

By now, the enemy had ploughed over all the runways, except one, on both the main and satellite airfields, making them basically useless. This runway was also observed to be ploughed over on the next day. On 27 March, some Fiats caused damage to three Ju 52s, a Vega Gull and a Rapide that were all parked at Jiggiga.

The main strip was again attacked on 29 March, but the Hurricanes operating off the satellite field defended it well, although Capt Theron had to carry out a forced landing after being hit in a Glycol pipe. His Hurricane 287 was attacked by the fighters and set on fire on the ground. In the meantime Lt Venter was fighting the remainder of the enemy aircraft and he managed to shoot down one of the three aircraft engaging him. Capt Frost had also by now taken off and shot down one of the CR.42s while they were trying to run for their base. One Valentia, a Ju 52

On the evening of 29 April 1941, the Staff at 2 Wing, of which 3 Squadron formed a part, calculated that the confirmed score for the squadron stood at 99 enemy aircraft destroyed in the air or on the ground. This would not hold out for long and the very next day, Capt Jack Frost added a S.79 shot down and a Fiat CR.32 left burning on the Gimma airfield to the total, to push the score past the 100 mark. Here the squadron can be seen chalking their total up on a fuselage of a CR.42 that the crew were busy restoring. The person with the chalk is the Officer Commanding, Maj Pretorius. Capt Jack Frost is standing second to the left from him, while Capt Theron is standing on the right hand edge of the photograph, with his cap on.

and a Hartebeest were destroyed on the main airfield in the attack, while Capt Theron's Hurricane was destroyed and that of Lt Venter badly shot up. Late in the afternoon, four Gladiators landed from Barbara and were attached to the squadron. The Gladiators were previously known as the Fighter Support Flight for the forward areas. On the last two days of the month, the squadron again re-deployed forward to Dire Dawa.

On 3 April, another friendly fire incident happened when Lt van Ginkel attacked a formation of Gladiators which was unidentified at the time. As he passed the Gladiator head-on he recognized the markings and broke off the attack. From 4 April onwards, the Hurricanes and Gladiators carried out strafing attacks on Addis Ababa, as well as escorting other bombers in the area on attacks on the airfield. On 5 April alone the squadron damaged and set fire to at least eight enemy aircraft on the various airfields that they attacked. The score on 6 April stood at two fighters shot down in aerial combat, three burnt on the ground, four bombers set alight on the ground with an additional ten aircraft severely damaged. Maj Niblock-Stuart left the squadron early in April while at Dire Dawa, and Maj J. D. Pretorius took over. On 9 April a further 13 enemy aircraft were destroyed during the various sorties on the day. During the remainder of April, a number of armed reconnaissance flights were carried out to different enemy airfields in a search for more targets but very few were encountered as operations moved into Southern Abyssinia. On 21 April, Lt Geraty flying a Gladiator shot down a Ca.133 when he scrambled on observing the aircraft in a distance while doing standby at Addis Ababa. The Officer Commanding, Maj Pretorius and Lt Howitson carried out strafing attacks on Gimma airfield on 24 April, when Lt Howitson was apparently shot down by intense anti-aircraft fire. Maj Pretorius observed a large flash during an attacking pass and could not find any trace of Lt Howitson thereafter. Searches on the next day showed no trace of him or his aircraft. He had to date accounted for at least 11 enemy aircraft as a result of aerial combats or ground strafing.

On the evening of 29 April, No. 2 Wing Operations Staff calculated the Squadron's total to be 99 enemy aircraft destroyed. On the very next day, Capt Frost encountered a lone S.79 and immediately shot it down, followed closely thereafter by a CR.32 left burning on the airfield at Gimma, for a new total of 101 enemy aircraft destroyed by 3 Squadron in a five-months period. Mr Hiram B. Blaufelt, an American War Correspondent, "African Mirror" and other pressmen filmed the squadron on 1 May just after the 101st victory was gained.

On 11 May, the composition of B-Flight, which until two days ago had been based at Kombolcha, was changed. The Flight handed its Hurricanes over to A-Flight and was in turn equipped with six Gladiators. The Flight would move to Algato in the Lake area and operate with 11 Squadron's Fairey Battles. During the afternoon of 12 May, Capt Theron started up a CR.42, which the squadron's crew had been building up over a period of time. After a few high speed runs he got airborne and flew around for a while demonstrating the fighter to the ground crew. The approach was done at a fairly high speed due to the lack of flaps of the CR.42 and the high altitude of the airfield. A go-around was performed with the intention of doing a few approaches to establish a safe landing speed. On the second go-around, the engine however cut when he was already about three-quarters across the airfield. At the end of the airfield was a wide ditch and one of the wheels hit the edge of this ditch during the landing causing the forced landing to end up with the aircraft a complete write-off. Capt Theron suffered cuts to both knees and slight facial injuries which was immediately attended to.

On 22 May, Maj Pretorius handed over Command of the Squadron to Maj van Pittius, who had already spent some time flying Gladiators with B-Flight at Algato. He was previously the Officer Commanding, 11 Squadron. Capt Frost was replaced as Flight Commander of A-Flight with Capt Clyde-Morley, while Capt Hayden-Thomas was also appointed as the new flight Commander of B-Flight. On 24 May, Lt Venter got a huge surprise when an isolated truck which he was attacking, blew up in his face. This was believed to be a booby trapped vehicle and orders were issued to pilots not to attack such isolated vehicles until further notice. Lt Venter managed a safe crash landing off his second approach with the damaged Hurricane back at Addis Ababa. He would sadly loose his life just a few days later on 3 June, when he went down in mountainous terrain in bad weather. On 11 June, the Algato Detachment returned to the main base at Addis Ababa, only to be posted back to Algato on 19 June, such was the fortunes of war.

2/Lt G. C. Hojem did not return from a Gladiator patrol flight over Gimma on the morning of 21 June and no news or sighting of him was again received. This was his first operational flight whilst on active duty. He arrived back at the squadron however, on 25 June. It appeared that he was forced to climb to a height of 18,000 ft (5,490 m) to get to Gimma through thick cloud and mist and then had to carry out a forced landing due to running out of fuel. He had to do the same again on the return flight. He landed safely in a field near a village, Buttagira, about 30 miles (48 km) from base and was assisted by the inhabitants to reach Algato safely again. This Gladiator was again crashed in an effort to recover it from the field he had forced landed in when it swung and overturned during the recovery effort. On 24 June, the Flight moved forward again to Gimma. 2/Lt Jacobs was detailed to escort the General Officer Commanding to Asmara on 26 June. After taking off from Kombolcha, he experienced engine trouble. He knew that the terrain ahead would offer very few forced landing opportunities and elected to return to Kombolcha. On landing there, the left hand wheel locked while he was correcting a swing. This caused the supporting bolts to shear off and the wheel left the axle. The left hand wing and the inter-plane struts were damaged. Two more Hurricanes were damaged during July 1941. 2/Lt R. Lilienfield overturned on landing at Addis Ababa with Hurricane 289/A, thus bringing and end to the third fighter flown by Capt Frost as a personal aircraft during his tour. Hurricane 292 was damaged while being flown by Lt A. C. Mitchell in a landing accident at Algato on 27 July. Towards the end of July, flying was severely hampered by adverse weather and cloud formations. The ground crew were again busy building up a Fiat CR.32 and CR.42, both of which were to be flown down to the Union to partake in a recruitment campaign which was planned to undertake a tour in the Union. These two enemy fighters would receive the SAAF serial numbers of 21 and 22 respectively. The CR.42 would still be serving during 1943.

On 28 July, orders were received to have as many aircraft as possible serviceable for the impending blitz to end the campaign with. A move from Kombolcha to Alomata was also expected soon. 3 Squadron had now, early in August 1941, almost seized to exist as a unit, as it only had three Hurricanes and two Gladiators serviceable in which operations could be carried out. On the first day of the attack on Gondor, the final Italian stronghold, Capt Hayden-Thomas was hit by anti-aircraft fire and had to crash land. Local inhabitants assisted him in successfully escaping from being captured.

By now the unit was in urgent need for spare propellers for the aircraft. Col Preller studied a propeller from a S.79 and decided to adapt one to fit a Gladiator. On the first test flight it was found to vibrate and a few inches were removed from each blade. As the Gladiators did not have

A line-up fo 3 Squadron's Mohawk Mk. IVs in East Africa, 1941. The famous "Fighting Wasp" emblem was again applied to the Mohawks in a slightly modified scheme. It was now applied in black to a light background, which appeared to be white.

Curtiss Mohawk Mk. IV, 2508, operated by 3 Squadron in East Africa. This was the Mohawk that Lt G. R. Jacobs was flying when he was killed in a crash on 20 November 1941. It appeared that he had stalled the Mohawk in a turn, did one and a half turns of a spin and dived into the ground.

equipment for variable pitch propellers, the blades were fixed in an intermediate position and further test flights proved successful. The aircraft used a bit of a longer ground run than an aircraft equipped with a standard propeller, but was much faster once airborne. Lt Mitchell was shot down on 26 August on a mission to Azozo, but survived the crash landing and eventually returned to Alamato.

Shortly afterwards, while based at Nanyuki, the squadron was re-equipped with a new aircraft type, namely the Mohawk Mk. IV. After a few weeks training the squadron returned to Alamato. With an advance Flight at Dabat, the squadron operated with great success over Gondar and Lake Tana area, using the Mohawks as fighter bombers.

The SAAF received 72 Mohawk aircraft. The first Mohawk, with British serial number AR636, was shipped to Takoradi on the Gold Coast. The aircraft made its first flight on 22 December 1940, crashing into the sea minutes later due to a seized engine. Major modifications were required to the engines. The first nine aircraft sent to Mombasa to re-equip 3 Squadron, during March 1941, all had unmodified engines. These engines had to be returned to Britain for modifications. On 13 July 1941, 20 modified Mohawks arrived at Mombasa. No. 3 Squadron was withdrawn to Nanyuki on 27 August 1941 for refit with the Mohawks.

Three of these aircraft were attached to 41 Squadron and, as "41 Squadron Detached Fighter Flight" under Capt Parsonson, were sent from Nairobi to the Vichy French border at Aiscia. Their target was a Savoia S.75, which was staging back and forth through Djibouti, bringing war material to the Italians. Attempts to intercept the Savoia failed and permission was granted on 23 September 1941 to attack the aircraft on the ground. Two attempts on 4 and 5 October 1941 failed, but a second raid on Djibouti on 5 October 1941 caught the Savoia on the ground. Captain Parsonson destroyed it with incendiary bullets.

During this month the unit was re-designated 3 Squadron, B-Flight. On 24 October 1941, 3 Squadron carried out tests at Nakuru of the modified bomb racks fitted to 12 Mohawks of the squadron. The fitting of the attachments to the bomb racks, so as to carry British bombs, was made necessary by the allocation of the Mohawks for the operations against Gondar. With the new racks the aircraft would be able to carry 20 lb High Explosives Mk. I and 20 lb Fragmentation Bombs. In the case of the Fragmentation Bombs, the modifications also provided for two types of bomb pistols. The attachments were designed by the Chief Armaments Officer, in collaboration with the Workshop Staff, RAF Eastleigh, where the racks were manufactured. On 3 November, the squadron had ten Mohawks available on A-Flight, while another five were serving on B-Flight.

On 8 November, three of the Mohawks operating from Alomata airfield, made an offensive reconnaissance of Sena and Areb. A total of 8,000 rounds of ammunition were fired at trenches and buildings in which five machine gun posts were silenced. On the next day three Mohawks carried out attacks on positions at Johannes in which 3,600 rounds of ammunition were fired and 400 lbs (181 kg) of bombs dropped in the attacks. This was to be followed later in the day by five aircraft who got airborne for attacks on positions near Sena, where direct hits were observed in the target area from 680 lbs of bombs that were dropped. On 10 November, three Mohawks attacked Sena and the hills South of Deva. They dropped 600 lbs (272 kg) of bombs and fired 9,000 rounds of ammunition. Four direct hits were reported on trenches and a tent and huts were set on fire. Three more Mohawks attacked positions at Ambazzo where direct hits were scored on huts and trenches. Two machine-gun posts were also silenced.

On 11 November, two Mohawks and a Hurricane attacked Ambazzo. Seven direct hits were scored on trenches, huts and machine-gun posts. The attacking aircraft experienced intense light machine-gun fire during their attacks. A further six Mohawks dropped 1,200 lbs (544 kg) of bombs and fired 12,700 rounds of ammunition on camps at Jangua and Coladiba. One gun post was silenced and nine direct hits were recorded, while light return fire was experienced. A third attack on the day by three Mohawks was carried out against Jangua in cooperation with three Hartebeeste from 41 Squadron. A direct hit was reported on a large tent, filled with troops and on a building. Eight further hits were recorded on trenches and one machine-gun post was silenced.

On 12 November one Mohawk and a Hurricane from 3 Squadron patrolled Azozo in order to attack a Savoia S.75 expected to arrive at Gondor early in the morning. The aircraft, however, did not arrive. Later in the day six Mohawks carried out the third and seventh waves of follow-up attacks in the advance along the Feroaber Ridge. On 14 November, two Mohawks and three Hartebeeste carried out attacks on Azozo and Coladiba. Four direct hits were recorded on a wireless station and one hit on a fort. Two Mohawks, armed with only full ammunition capacity for all guns and without any bombs, rendezvoused with four Wellesleys over Adua to search for signs of 15 German aircraft that were supposedly reported to have landed 130 km from Asmara, near Adua. Nothing was found and the aircraft returned, while one Wellesley spun in due to engine failure during the flight, killing the pilot, S/Ldr Illsley.

In preparation for the final attacks on enemy positions at Gondor, a continuous air attack on the enemy positions from Ambazzo to Azozo, was planned for 17 November. Three Mohawks carried out a dive-bombing attack on Deva, while six Mohawks attacked targets at Azozo and Gondar. Three machine-gun posts at Azozo were silenced. A further attack was made by three Mohawks on Deva and Daflecha. One direct hit on an anti-aircraft post and five direct hits on trenches were scored. An ammunition dump was strafed and it blew up.

A further continuous air attack was ordered on positions in the Feroaber and Kulkaber Pass positions on 20 November and 18 Mohawks in total partook in the various attacks on the day. A total of 15,248 lbs (6,907 kg) of bombs were dropped and 55,030 rounds of ammunition were fired. Direct hits on trenches, machine-gun posts, huts and other buildings, including fortifications, were recorded. In addition, several fires were started. Mohawk 2508 crashed on take-off and the pilot, Lt G. R. Jacobs, was killed. It appeared that he had stalled the aircraft in a turn, did one and a half turns of a spin and dived into the ground.

The next day, four Mohawks made an offensive reconnaissance over Azozo, Daflecha and Chelga. Direct hits were scored on entrenchments and buildings at Azozo and Gorgora. Some fuel drums were also set alight by machine gun fire. The enemy was, on 23 November, still occupying two forts in Gorgora on the East and West of the road, on high ground to the north of the village. On the next day three Mohawks attacked enemy concentrations in Torelli's camp, between Gondar and Azozo. The attacks were followed by attacks with Hartebeeste on the same targets.

In preparation for forthcoming attacks by the own ground forces on Azozo, two Mohawks and a Hartebeest carried out reconnaissance flights on 26 November. Specific targets included enemy gun positions in action and any troops moving Southbound. During attacks on various targets hits were scored on huts, tents and trenches, while two machine-gun posts were silenced and a building destroyed.

During their service with 3 Squadron, the bomb racks on the Mohawks were modified to carry British bombs. The aircraft were typically armed with ten 20-lb bombs per flight in the attacks against the last Italian stronghold at Gondar. Each fighter could thus carry 200 lb of bombs per flight. The photograph shows a Mohawk armed with five bombs under the left hand wing. Note how the camouflage pattern of the wing upper surfaces stretches round to the lower surface of the wing.

Mohawk Mk. IV, 2529, of 3 Squadron, photographed during December 1941. This Mohawk was flown back from Nairobi to the Union by Lt Leisegang, in the formation lead by Capt Parsonson. The route was from Eastleigh to Dodoma, to Kasama, to Lusaka, to Bulawayo to Zwartkops Air Station.

On 27 November, 16 Hartebeeste and eight Mohawks dropped a total of 21,650 lbs (9,808 kg) of bombs on Gondar. Own armour and troops were seen to enter Gondar at 1030 hrs in the morning. On this day, General Guglielmo Ciro Nasi surrendered the last Italian garrison in East Africa unconditionally.

The Operations Instruction on 30 November, announcing the final surrender of all the enemy forces in the Gondar area, was received. The order instructed that 3 Squadron would be returning to the Union of South Africa, thereby ending their participation in the East African Campaign, with the exception of B-Flight, still operating from Aiscia in operations against French Somaliland. The personnel, transport and equipment at Alomata were to proceed to Massawa on the afternoon of 2 December 1941, for shipment to the Union. The aircraft were all to be flown to the Union and a Movement Table would be issued later. One Flight of 41 Squadron was tasked to re-condition their equipment at Addis Ababa and then to move forward to Aiscia to replace B-Flight, 3 Squadron. By December most of 3 Squadron was back at Nairobi, with B-Flight still serving at Aiscia. Shortly hereafter, the Mohawks were returned to the Union, to be used as training aircraft.

On 10 December No. 2 Wing SAAF in East Africa issued a No. 2 Wing Operation Instruction, stating that Mohawks from 3 Squadron were urgently required in the Union for training purposes. The intention of the order was to fly nine Mohawks from Eastleigh to Zwartkops Air Station by pilots of 3 Squadron. The aircraft would depart in two waves of five and four aircraft respectively. All aircraft were to depart on 11 December. Maj Lucas, the Officer Commanding, 3 Squadron, would lead the first five aircraft, while Capt Parsonson would lead the second wave of four aircraft. The route to follow would be Eastleigh – Dodoma – Kasama – Lusaka – Bulawayo – Zwartkops Air Station. In case of bad weather the airfields at Arusha, Mbeya, Ndola, Broken Hill, Salisbury and Pietersburg were also available.

Capt Parsonson flew Mohawk 2556 during this ferry, leading Lt van der Merwe in 2539, Lt Leisegang in Mohawk 2529, and Lt Lillianfield in Mohawk 2511 from Nairobi to Zwartkops Air Station. These two formations were followed on 13 December by three more Mohawks from Eastleigh, under command of Lt Wildsmith. On 23 December, a special notice was issued, reminding pilots of the danger of loading oversize baggage in the wireless locker in the rear fuselage of the Mohawks, as these items were causing damage to the radio in the equipment bay. During January 1942, a number of Mohawks, assembled at Eastleigh, were delivered as follows; five Mohawks to Zwartkops Air Station on 15 January, two Mohawks to Aiscia on 28 January 1942 and three Mohawks to Aden on 30 January 1942.

After the fall of Gondar and the cessation of hostilities in Italian East Africa the squadron moved to Asmara where it disbanded after a short stay. From Asmara the personnel proceeded by road to Masawa from where they embarked for the Union. The squadron was eventually reformed in the Union under leadership of Capt C. A. van Vliet and left for the Middle East on 16 December 1942, aboard the ship "Nieuw Amsterdam", from which vessel it disembarked at Suez on New Year's Day 1943.

4 Squadron

This Squadron was initially established on 19 September 1939 in Durban, The Union Defence Force Routine Order was dated 24 June 1939. The unit was designated as No. 4 Bomber-Fighter Squadron SAAF, but the name was changed on the same order to No. 4 (City of Durban) Bomber-Fighter Squadron SAAF.

4 Squadron took over the equipment and personnel from the Natal Air Training School. The first Officer Commanding was Maj B. G. Viljoen, with 18 officers and 34 other ranks. The squadron's initial aircraft consisted of one flight of five Hawker Furies, one flight of six Hawker Harts and one flight of seven Hawker Harts.

Just before the official promulgation date, Maj B. G. Viljoen and one flight equipped with seven of the Hawker Harts returned to Zwartkops Air Station. Capt A. J. Mossop assumed command on 16 September and was followed-up by Maj J. G. Davis on 26 September 1939.

The squadron was engaged with Coastal Defence duties. Its aircraft carried out coastal patrols for a short period and a stand-by flight was kept on 24-hour duty for emergencies. Shortly afterwards the squadron returned to Zwartkops Air Station and the aircraft became unserviceable due to bearing faults. Most of the pilots then went on training courses and some were transferred to No. 2 Fighter Squadron at Durban during October and November of that year.

In December 1939, the squadron was disbanded. The unit, however, reformed at Waterkloof Air Station on 24 March 1941 under the leadership of Maj G. Ogilvie-Watson. The promulgation took place in the form of Air Directorate Part 1 Order No. 44 of 1941 dated 21 March 1941. Lt L. B. Gillett was detailed by the Operational Command HQ, Waterkloof Air Station, to assume duties as acting Adjutant pending the arrival of the rest of the personnel for the squadron. The squadron was constituted as a fighter squadron and the unit would comprise of a Headquarters and three flights. The personnel would total 182, including all ranks. On 31 March 1941, Maj B. B. F. Russell reported for duty and assumed duties as Administrative Officer of the squadron. Between 2 and 17 April, the personnel were given embarkation leave.

Seven officers and 218 men (including 60 personnel for 16 Squadron) under Lt Masters

A line-up of some of the Curtiss Mohawk Mk. IVs used by 4 Squadron at the OTU at Nakuru. The closest aircraft in line, 2508, was eventually lost in a crash in action at Alomata on 20 November 1941, while flown by Lt G. R. Jacobs of 3 Squadron. The second Mohawk in line, 2510, survived the East African Campaign and served again in the Union.

Hawker Furies of 4 Squadron at the Operational Training Unit based at Nakuru, during 1941. The closest aircraft is Fury 205. The unit operated the Hawker Fury and Hawker Audax before converting to Mohawks in June 1941.

embarked on the S.S. "Dalia" in Durban for Mombasa on 19 April 1941. The unit was now en route to Nakuru, Kenya. On 22 April, Capts Moodie and Kriel (Flight Commanders), Capt Hamelberg (Medical Officer), Lt Reeson (Equipment Officer) and 2/Lts Hope and Airey arrived by air at Nakuru. The aircraft were flown from the Union to Kenya via Northern Rhodesia.

The squadron personnel arrived at Mombasa on 26 April from where it moved forward by train to Nakuru on 28 April 1941. They arrived at the base on the same day and were met by Squadron Leader Kinnaer, the Officer Commanding of the station. The new Officer Commanding, 4 Squadron, Maj Barrett, arrived on 2 May 1941 after making arrangements concerning the establishment at Nairobi. On 4 May, the first Mohawk for the squadron was flown across from Eastleigh to Nakuru by Capt Moodie. On 10 May, a number of pilots arrived for the squadron, including Lts Clarkson, Wildsmith, Visser, Baker, Bosman, Harrison and 2/Lts du Plessis and Duff-Richardson. The Engineering Officer, Lt Booyse, also reported for duty. On 12 May the unit formed into three Flights, namely Headquarters Flight, A-Flight under Capt Kriel (Lts Bosman, Baker, Clarkson and Harrison and 2/Lt Duff-Richardson) and B-Flight under Capt Moodie (Lts Wildsmith and Visser and 2/Lts Airey, du Plessis and Anderson).

The squadron was equipped with Hawker Fury and Audax aircraft and training commenced on 12 May. These aircraft were taken over from 2 Squadron. The training included lectures on the Mohawk, presented by Capt Moodie. On 14 May a demonstration of Air-Cooperation was given by the squadron, cooperating with the 26th East African Infantry Brigade. The demonstration included low flying machine gun attacks and bombing attacks with flour bags. On the next day air-to-ground communications using the "T-Panel" and message dropping and message pick-up were demonstrated.

On 17 May 1941, Capt Moodie lead six Furies and three Audaxes in the first 4 Squadron Formation flight. On 20 May, the squadron started with fighter tactics training and quarter-astern, astern and quarter-frontal attacks were practised. Maj Barrett was transferred to 21 Squadron on 26 May, as the amended Fighter Squadron establishment did not allow for a Major in his position as Unit Adjutant. He was replaced in the position by Lt D. C. Mitchell Baker from the Air Reception Depot at Nairobi.

Fourteen Mohawks were flown from Eastleigh to Nakuru between 6 and 19 June 1941, with strict instructions that no aircraft was to be flown more than 25 hours and that all aerobatic flying were forbidden. Seven new pilots joined between 7 and 10 June, including 2/Lts A. W. Alder, R. E. Chadwick, W. M. Copeland, V. A. Greenberg, C. G. Leisegang, W. S. B. Stevenson and D. W. Golding.

Flying with the Mohawks eventually begun on 10 June and on the same day, four more pilots arrived for duty. They were 2/Lts S. R. Bass-

A Mohawk accident suspected to have happened during the training of 4 Squadron pilots at Nakuru, Kenya in 1941. Note how the upper surface camouflage colours wrapped around the leading edge of the wing and cowling lip. Note the dark painted wheel hub, believed to be either red or blue, the traditional colours used by the first two Flights of a squadron. 4 Squadron operated with three Flights at the time, namely a HQ Flight, A- and B-Flights.

A line-up of the Curtiss Mohawk fighters used by 4 Squadron during their training at 70 OTU, Nakuru, East Africa. Flying on the type started on 10 June 1941.

ingthwaite, E. N. Colman, B. A. Robertshaw and R. A. B. Thorpe. The unit again changed an Adjutant when Lt Mitchell Baker, who was transferred to Mombasa, was replaced by Lt H. C. Morrison, transferred in from 40 Squadron.

On 25 June, Capt Kriel and Lt Morrison dispatched in Audax 7549 to Nairobi to make arrangements for a proposed move of the unit to Nanyuki. They were, however, forced to stay at Nairobi due to engine trouble and could only continue the next day. It was decided to return six of the Mohawks to Eastleigh, as it was undesirable to have more aircraft than necessary exposed in the open at Nanyuki, where there was no hanger available. A surprise message received on 4 July, stated that the authority for the move to Nanyuki had been withdrawn and the Officer Commanding and the Adjutant immediately left by vehicle to Nairobi to interview the Air Officer Commanding. They obtained the authority again and proceeded to Nanyuki to make final arrangements.

The Advance Party of 4 Squadron moved across on 9 July, with the remainder of the squadron following the next day. While the unit was housed in barracks at Nakuru, everything now was under canvas, with the camp situated on the edge of the aerodrome, about 4 miles (6 km) from the village of Nanyuki.

The unit experienced a loss on 11 July, when 2/Lt H. B. Stevenson, with Capt Curtis of the Bomber Brigade Maintenance Corps, crashed in a Hawker Hart. It seemed that the aircraft had struck a tree on a hill, due to the pilot flying low in heavy misty conditions. On 11 July, the aircraft flown by Capt Moodie and Cpl Kohler also disappeared in the heavy mist conditions. They however, reported to Fort Hall the next day, having walked some 30 miles (48 km) through the jungle. It transpired that they had also experienced engine failure and the aircraft was completely destroyed in the subsequent forced landing in the jungle. The wreckage was completely covered by trees and could not be observed by search parties.

The squadron remained at Nanyuki until the end of August, while continuing their training using the Mohawk and Audax. At last on 25 August, orders were received that the unit would leave for Egypt. The squadron departed Nanyuki by train on 1 September 1941 and on 3 September they left East Africa by boat (S.S. "Ascarius") from Mombasa, for the Middle East, arriving at Suez on 16 September 1941. From here they travelled by train to Amriya. On 19 and 20 September the unit was transferred to Aboukir. Only on 2 October, an Advance Party was sent out to RAF Station Amriya and the balance of the squadron followed the next day. Here they were equipped with and converted to Tomahawks and training began immediately. The Flight Commanders were posted to 2 Squadron and three senior pilots were posted to 1 Squadron to gain experience with these units. The unit would soon be involved in the fight in the Northern Desert.

Mohawk Mk. IV, 2531, was one of the aircraft used by 4 Squadron during their training at Nakuru, East Africa. This aircraft was finished in Dark Earth and Dark Green upper surfaces, with SAAF Sky Blue lower surfaces and carried standard period roundels. Note the underwing bomb racks and landing light below the left hand wing. Also note the shape of the lower finish below the cowling lip.

41 Squadron

Squadron served as an Army Cooperation Squadron during the East African Campaign, flying Hawker Hartebeest aircraft. On completion of the campaign in December 1941, the unit was kept in East Africa with the aim of converting the squadron to a full fighter squadron. Their service in the Army Cooperation role will thus not be covered in this volume, as the primary discussions herein go about the SAAF Fighter Squadrons in East Africa. This discussion will only cover their East African service, post the East African Campaign and before being deployed to the Middle East.

During January 1942, the squadron deployed to a new camp that was set up at Gilgal and it was surmised that the unit would be based here for a period of time. On 25 May 1942, Maj H. Mc G. Ingles, the Officer Commanding, 41 Squadron, was informed that the proposed reorganisation of the squadron to a Fighter Squadron had been agreed to. This agreement would cancel the planned transfer of 3 Squadron to East Africa. The Squadron would receive 16 Hawker Hurricanes to arm two Flights within two weeks and two further Flights were to be armed with Hurricanes as soon as more aircraft were available. In the interim a Hartebeest Flight with nine aircraft was to be maintained by the squadron for cooperation with the army. All other Hartebeest aircraft were to be returned to the Union.

On 1 July 1942, the unit was located with the Headquarters Flight at Nairobi, A-Flight at Giggiga, and B- and C-Flights at Gilgil. The Flights all continued to operate on the Hawker Hartebeest. A number of photo reconnaissance flights were made during the month, including areas of French Somaliland. Some photo mosaics were also flown over some of the target areas such as Dikkil and Ali Sabiet. The squadron also received a number of new replacement pilots during the month. On 11 July, the Headquarters Flight at Nairobi were given notice to leave the Civil Aerodrome within 48 hours and they decided to move to Gilgil. During August a number of flights were made to Dire Dawa to inspect the bomb dump that was present there. The new pilots had started their training and received lectures on Army Cooperation work. Some dummy attacks were carried out over the positions of the 4/4 Kenyan African Rifles positions as part of the training.

Exercises were held with the East African Command, operating from MacKinnon Rd, flights being undertaken for the 26th and 28th Brigades respectively. Five crews and Hartebeeste partook in these exercises. The exercises were completed by 3 September 1942 and on 12 September the aircraft took off for the return to base via Eastleigh. On arrival at Eastleigh, two Hartebeeste were left in the workshops there for repairs. The Officer Commanding was notified

The crew of a 41 Squadron Hartebeest posing for a photograph with their ground crew.

Hawker Hartebeest 818 of 41 Squadron was still recorded serviceable and operational on the Squadron strength during April 1942.

that there was a Hurricane awaiting allotment to 41 Squadron at Eastleigh.

This was the first sign since 25 May 1942 that the unit would now eventually become a fighter squadron. After lunch the remaining three Hartebeeste and the Hurricane took off for Gilgil. In the afternoon of 8 September, a Dakota arrived at Giggiga, with eight American Army Air Corps officers on board as passengers. They inspected both the main and satellite airfields at Giggiga. During the last week of September, Hartebeeste 826 and 868 were flown to Hargeisha to carry out standby duties for anti-submarine patrols against Japanese submarines operating in the Gulf of Aden.

On 10 October, the squadron was advised that their Hurricanes would arrive from approximately 23 October 1942 onwards. On 12 October, the Squadron OC, Maj Ingles, was tragically killed in a flying accident at 71 Operational Training Unit. The Squadron was advised of a move to Mombasa and on 20 October, the advance party under command of Capt Chapman left for Port Reitz aerodrome to prepare camp there.

On the afternoon of 23 October, five Hurricanes and a Blenheim arrived at Gilgil, under command of Capt Alexander. A large crowd, including the whole of 41 Squadron, witnessed the arrival. Another five Hurricanes arrived on the morning of 24 October, with two Hurricanes departing for Eastleigh in the afternoon to have the long range tanks removed. During the landing at Eastleigh on the morning of 25 October, one aircraft (HV486) was badly damaged on landing. On inspection of the new Hurricanes, it was found that the tyres were badly worn, most likely as a result of using a tar-runway at their previous base. On the 26th, two more

A line-up of 41 Squadron Hartebeeste before an operation in East Africa. Note the underwing bomb racks.

Hurricane Mk. IIBs, HV515/J and HV514/P of 41 Squadron, formed the 6th Flight during 41 Squadron's move from Gilgal to Port Reitz Airfield, Mombasa on 10 December 1942. Both aircraft had their long range tanks fitted and still carried the distemper ferry markings on the rear fuselages and tailplanes.

Hurricanes departed to Eastleigh to have the long range tanks removed. Four more left and returned from Eastleigh on the 29th, for the removal of the tanks, while on 30 October, one aircraft, HV480, made a safe landing when the canopy hood had been torn off during flight, damaging the empennage in the process.

During the first week of November, a number of practise interception sorties were flown from Gilgil with the Hurricanes against Bostons and Bisleys based at Nanyuki. The pilots also carried out formation practise flights and cross country navigation flights. Hurricane HV500 was damaged at Nanyuki on 12 October when an Anson which was taxying in, collided with it. Fairly extensive damage was caused to the tail end and empennage. Three more aircraft arrived for the Squadron during the last week of November 1942. On the last day of the month, the squadron was advised by the OC, Maj Haydon-Thomson an impending move to the coast. The unit left Gilgil on 8 December, by train and by road.

On 10 December 1942, the Squadron arrived at RAF Station Port Reitz, Mombasa. Shortly after arriving there, four Hurricanes were fitted with long range tanks and these were tested on 26 December 1942. These aircraft were HV501,

The 41 Squadron Hawker Hurricane Mk. IIBs on their arrival at Gilgal, during the last week of October 1942. The photograph shows HV490/X fitted with the long range tanks and the white distemper paint from the ferry flight across Africa from Takoradi, to the East Coast, still visible on the rear fuselage and tailplanes. Note the rough application of the distemper paint. The aircraft were all flown to Eastleigh in the next few days where the long range tanks were removed.

This photograph shows Hurricane Mk. IIB HV490/X on the left, with Hurricane HV509/K on the right hand side of the photograph. Note the rough and different application of the distemper paint between the various aircraft. Hurricane K has the paint applied almost in a band around the rear fuselage, while the application on Hurricane X extends up on to the vertical fin, but not around the fuselage.

HV498, HV500 and HV514. They departed on 27 December under command of Capt Chapman, to a "secret destination". Ten personnel had also departed in the preceding week to "secret destinations". The other three pilots were Lts Aitchison, Smith and Leisagang. The aircraft returned on the last day of the year, having completed their mission. A newspaper published on 30 December 1942 announced that French Somaliland had been handed over, thus covering the "secret destination" that the members of the squadron went to!

Maj Hayden-Thomas arrived back from the Union on 11 April 1943 to take over Command of the squadron. He and Maj Hughes addressed the squadron about the new "V" Oath for service anywhere in the world, as the original oath taken by the members only covered service in Africa. Soon afterwards Lt Col Galgut arrived from Nairobi and informed the squadron that all squadrons were being moved out of East Africa. 41 Squadron arrived in the Middle East on 6 May 1943 and started training on Hurricane Mk. IIB. On 12 May 1943, the squadron found itself at Shandur (North Africa). The unit had thus effectively spent another year and a half in East Africa, on conclusion of the East African Campaign.

Hawker Hurricane Mk. IIB with code letter H leads a line-up of four 41 Squadron aircraft. The white distemper paint has been removed and the aircraft are again fitted with long range tanks. This photograph could be depicting the four Hurricanes which were used for the operation in French Somaliland during the last few days of December 1942.

41 Fighter Flight

41 Squadron Detached Fighter Flight

The unit was formed with the aim of sealing off the border of French Somaliland. The crew were first introduced to Mohawks on 1 September 1941. After one week of practise they moved over to Eastleigh Aerodrome, Nairobi on 8 September. The pilots were Maj H. Borckenhagen, appointed as the Officer Commanding, Capt J. Parsonson Second in Command, 2/Lt P. Strong and 2/Lt D. Gazzard. During the week of training, Capt Jack Parsonson flew Mohawks 2519, 2510, 2517 and 2520, all based at 70 Operational Training Unit at Nakuru. Of these aircraft, he was involved in a crash with 2510 on 2 September 1941. The pilots continued training and flights between Nakuru and Eastleigh in the period 11 September until 14 September 1941. In this training period Capt Parsonson flew Mohawks 2504, 2503 and 2512. They were finally allocated three Mohawks and eleven groundcrew members.

On 11 September, four men left by Ju 52 for Aiscia. 2/Lt Gazzard crashed owing to engine failure while coming in to land, but was unhurt. On the next day, the OC went down with malaria and was replaced by Capt Snyman as Officer Commanding. On 14 Spetember, 2/Lt Strong over-ran the aerodrome and crashed into a bank, after a flapless landing due to system failure. He was unhurt. The next morning, Lt Turner (who had been added as pilot), 2/Lt Gazzard, the remaining seven men and an American, Pail Carpenter, the representative of the Curtiss Airplane Works, left for Aiscia by Ju 52, where the unit would fall under operational control of A.H.Q. Aden. On 16 September, Capts Snyman and Parsonson and 2/Lt Strong left with the three allocated Mohawks, routing from Nairobi to Yavello on the first leg of the journey to Aiscia. The three aircraft were serials 2513, 2522 and 2514.

On 17 September 1941, while climbing through cloud outbound from Yavello, the flight members lost sight of each other. Capt Snyman eventually arrived at Aiscia at 1500 hrs, while Capt Parsonson returned to Yavello flying 2522, where he spent two days looking for Capt Snyman and 2/Lt Strong, whom he thought had crashed. 2/Lt Strong had disappeared while doing a wide circuit of Yavello aerodrome, Capt Parsonson arrived at Aiscia on 18 September and 2/Lt Gazzard, who was on standby, got airborne and escorted him inbound. The routing from Yavello was via Algato and Awash to Aiscia.

Lt Turner got airborne at about 0730 hrs on 19 September, after two enemy aircraft which had been sighted. They however altered course in the direction of Jibuti. Capt Snyman also fell ill with malaria, while the remaining three pilots continued standby and patrol duties, with Capt Parsonson completing a test flight on Mohawk 2522. On 25 September, word was received from 2/Lt Strong, that he was at Mega and was awaiting fuel from Yuvello. Capt Parsonson again test flew Mohawk 2522 on completion of the inspection on 26 September. Later in the day he flew a patrol flight in Mohawk 2514. The next day, during a test flight with 2514, he

A line-up of the Curtiss Mohawks operated by 70 Operational Training Unit at Nakuru during the period when the Detached Fighter Flight members did their conversions. Mohawk 2503, the nearest aircraft, was one of the aircraft flown by Capt Parsonson.

crashed the aircraft, due to engine problems experienced.

On 28 September, 2/Lt Gazzard received promotion to lieutenant and in the afternoon he left for Dire Dawa with Capt Snyman and Mr Carpenter who were going to Nairobi. Capt Parsonson flew an air-to-ground practise flight the morning with 2522. The next day a message was received that 2/Lt Strong had crashed at Mega on take-off, when his controls had apparently jammed when he was about 100 ft (30 m) up. The remaining pilots meanwhile kept up the standby duties and patrols on a daily basis (Capt Parsonson flying 2522), while Lt Turner left for Dire Dawa and Nairobi on 1 October 1941, to go and fetch another aircraft.

In the afternoon, two Ju 86 aircraft from 35 Flight arrived from Gondor, to take over the patrol reconnaissance duties that the Mohawks had carried out to date. They were joined by four Vincents from Aden, as well as a third Ju 86 from Nairobi. Two of the Vincents would be staying on at base, as communication aircraft.

After receiving word that a Savoia S.75 was present at Jibuti, Capt Parsonson flying Mohawk 2522, on 5 October, found the aircraft on the airfield and set it on fire with two strafing attacks. By 8 October, they had still not received any word from Lts Turner and Judd (who had been sent to replace 2/Lt Strong) who had to bring two Mohawks from Nairobi. On 14 October, word was received that one Mohawk had reached Yavello, but that Lt Turner had landed short of the base due to a fuel shortage, fortunately with no damage to the aircraft. On 16 October, word was received that the unit was now officially renamed as B-Flight 3 Squadron, from the previous day onwards.

3 Squadron B-Flight

On the same day, a signal was received, that the two Mohawks had left Yavello for Aiscia, but had turned back due to weather. They eventually arrived at Aiscia on 19 September, where the two aircraft first had to be serviced after the long flight to Aiscia. This was completed on 20 October and they both started patrol flights on 21 October. On 22 October, Capt Parsonson was ordered by Air Headquarters East Africa to return to Nanyuki and he departed on 26 October in a Ju 86 flown by Lt Paterson.

On 23 October, Lt Gazzard crashed while taking off, when a whirlwind hit the Mohawk, just as the tail was rising. The aircraft was swung into a small petrol dump. Lt Gazzard received a nasty burn on his left arm when the petrol burst into flames. The rudder and elevators of the aircraft were also burnt and the undercarriage and propeller were badly damaged. Some members from 35 Flight were attached to B-Flight 3 Squadron on 1 November 1941, while the officers departed for Nairobi, via Mombasa. They arrived on 24 November at Nairobi. On 2 November, Lt Gazzard left in Mohawk 2513 for Addis Ababa to collect Mohawk 2542 in exchange. Lts Judd and Turner meanwhile continued their patrol duties and standby duties.

An Operations Order were issued by the Air Headquarters East Africa on 3 November for the movement of three Mohawks under Lt Wildsmith in order to complete the establishment of 3 Squadron Flights. These flights were to take place on 12 November. Mohawk 2511 would be flown by himself from Eastleigh to Alomata, while 2/Lt Arbuthnot was to pilot Mohawk 2542 from Eastleigh to Addis Ababa. He was to hand over the second aircraft at Addis Ababa to the Officer Commanding, 18 Air Depot, and then take over Mohawk 2513, which he then had to deliver to Alomata. Lt A. C. Mitchell would fly Mohawk 2545 to Alomata. On arrival at Alomata, all three pilots would report to the Officer Commanding, 3 Squadron, for duty. Orders were confirmed on 4 November that the following actions were to be taken on encountering Vichy aircraft, operating outside the French Somaliland border. On the first occasion, warning bursts were to be fired out of range of the offending aircraft, using the outboard guns only. On subsequent occasions of infringement of the border, offensive action to shoot down the offender was to be taken. The outboard guns of the Mohawks had to be loaded with the maximum permissible proportions of tracer ammunition. Own aircraft were not to fly within five miles of the border of French Somaliland. These restrictions were to be imposed on Air Detachments operating with 28 Brigade.

Three RAF Vincents arrived on 11 November 1941, to take over the patrol duties from the Mohawks, but B-Flight was advised to keep a Mohawk at the ready, in case an enemy aircraft landed at Jibuti on 12 and 13 November. On 12 November, a signal was received that two Mohawks were arriving at Addis Ababa, but B-Flight was uncertain as to whether the aircraft were allocated to them, or not. On 14 November, another signal was received, indicating that Lt A. C. Mitchell had crashed in Mohawk 2545, while taking off. This accident appeared to have happened on 12 November and it was reported that the pilot did a climbing turn at too slow a speed near the ground after take-off. The aircraft stalled and dived into the ground where after it burnt out and the pilot was killed instantly. A third message requested that Lt Gazzard

Mohawk Mk. IV 2514 was flown by Capt Parsonson on a morning patrol on 25 September 1941 from Aiscia. During a second patrol flight on 26 September, he had to carry out a crash landing due to engine problems experienced on the same aircraft.

be picked up at Dire Dawa on 18 November. On 17 November, a signal was received stating that the Mohawk, which Lt Gazzard should have taken, were flown to Alomata by Lt Joubert. Lt Gazzard was however, picked up at Dire Dawa on 18 November, by Flt Lt Adams in a Vincent. Mohawk 2542 arrived during the morning, in company of a Hartebeest which returned the pilot to Alomata.

Lt Geldenhuys arrived at the Detachment on 1 December 1941, with some plugs and push-rod spares for the Mohawks. He advised the personnel that the remainder of 3 Squadron were leaving for the Union on 2 December and that the Detachment should also go as soon as Jibuti had fallen. For the next few days patrols were carried out with at least two aircraft, but sometimes with all three. On 9 December, both Mohawks 2542 and 2528 were on standby.

On 11 December, Lt Gazzard was just taking off when a Potez 63 from Jibuti dived over the camp. Lt Gazzard saw it and chased after it. The rear gunner fired on him, where after he replied and smoke was seen to come from the port engine of the Potez. The aircraft escaped by diving into some low cloud. Regular patrols and standbys were carried out and on 26 December 1941, Lt Turner was hit by anti-aircraft fire in the fuselage and tailplane, when he was flying past the Vichy French post at Loyada. The Mohawk was not badly damaged. On the same day, Lt Gazzard left for Nairobi in Mohawk 2522.

B-Flight was relieved by C-Flight from 41 Squadron and then also returned to the Union.

Meanwhile, on 3 November, the situation at Eastleigh was reported as that all Mohawk aircraft were now modified in accordance with Modification 30. This consisted of drilling two holes in the Clarke's viscosity valve. Previous cases of engine failure, causing several forced landings, led to grounding of the fleet. A local modification that was used initially were cancelled when Modification 30 was received and the grounding of the Mohawks were cancelled on completion of Modification 30.

On 7 November it was reported in the Operations Record Book East Africa, that modifications were carried out on the wireless sets of certain of the Mohawks at RAF Station Eastleigh, with the work completed on 3 November 1941. The modification of all Mohawks in respect of the oil system was also completed on 3 November. All Mohawks had been grounded, following several forced landings. These included a successful forced landing on Eastleigh aerodrome after an engine cut on 6 November. The grounding was cancelled on the completion of the modification. On 7 November, Mohawks recently erected at Eastleigh, were again grounded due to two cases of big-end bearing failure. The grounding was pending the investigation by the American Engine Representative.

On 23 November, Eastleigh reported another case of big-end bearing failure in a Mohawk. This happened on 13 November and the pilot carried out a successful forced landing on the Eastleigh aerodrome. On 23 November, a case was found where a celluloid blanking disc was left in place on an oil pipe inlet port. The disc was damaged, thus allowing oil to pass through. All Mohawk aircraft being erected at Eastleigh, immediately had the oil systems inspected for similar defects.

On 7 December it was reported that the Mohawks at Eastleigh were experiencing problems, with the airscrews surging in constant speed. The assistance of C. A. Thomson of the Curtiss Propeller Division had been requested.

On 6 February 1942, a new document containing Modification 3 on Wright Cyclone Engines, as fitted to the Mohawks, were issued. The modification, which was embodied at Hartlebury in engines of 205 Group, was found to have light alloy spacer rings fitted to the master rod in lieu of steel spacer rings, causing failure. The group was requested to remove a cylinder and inspect all Cyclone engines fitted in Mohawk aircraft.

On 19 February 1942, Mohawk 2521 was flown from Eastleigh to Zwartkops Air Station by Lt du Rose while on 7 April 1942, Mohawk 2534 was to be flown to Zwartkops Air Station by Lt George. A final Mohawk from Eastleigh, was delivered to the Union, on 26 April 1942, thereby ending the SAAF service period of the type in East Africa.

Aircraft finishes

Hawker Fury Mk. I and II

The first seven Hawker Furies were delivered to South Africa during September 1936. The Furies carried serial numbers 200 to 206 and were equipped with Kestrel VI engines, the same as in the Fury Mk. II, tropical radiators and oil coolers. They initially served with the Central Flying School, before being allocated to 2 Bomber/Fighter Squadron at Waterkloof Air Station in early 1939. When 1 Squadron deployed to Nairobi in May 1940, six of these Furies were crated and shipped to East Africa onboard the S.S. "Takliwa" on 26 May 1940. The Furies arrived at Mombasa and were assembled there. During August 1940, the unit received additional Furies from ex-RAF stock and these were Mk. Is in a well-used condition. Another 16 Furies were received during October 1940 and January 1941. On 4 August 1940, the strength was reduced by two aircraft, when Lt B. R. Dimmock in Fury 202 and Lt G. L. McBride in 204 collided during a training flight. Both members managed to parachute to safety with minor injuries.

On their delivery in South Africa, the original seven Furies were finished in silver doped fabric panels with the metal panels being left in a highly polished natural metal finish. The serial numbers were initially applied in Black to the rear fuselages only, but were later added to the rudders as well. The serial numbers were also applied to both lower wing surfaces in Black, with that below the right hand wing reading correct when the aircraft was approaching the observer, and that below the left hand wing reading correct when the aircraft was departing from the observer. The Furies carried Type A roundels in Orange, White and Blue on the rear fuselages, above the upper wings and below the lower wings. The centre circle was finished in Orange with the outer circle in Blue. No fin flashes were applied in this period. The normal stenciling was applied in Black to the various sections of the aircraft. From the available period photographs it would appear that the front of the propeller blades and the hub were painted in a light grey colour, with the back of the blades being painted in Black.

Before the six remaining Furies were crated and sent to East Africa, they were re-painted at the Aircraft and Artillery Repair Depot in Rob-

Hawker Fury 201 at Zwartkops Air Station. The Fury is finished in silver doped fabric and polished natural metal sections. The serial number was now applied in Black to the rear fuselage and to the rudder as well. Type A roundels were painted in Orange/White/Blue on the rear fuselages, above the upper wing and below the lower wing. The Orange was in the centre of the roundels with the Blue being the outer circle. The polished metal areas can clearly be seen in the photograph, compared to the dull silver doped areas of the fuselage and wings.

Hawker Fury 203 and one of the ex-RAF Fury Mk. Is photographed during their take-off roll at Husseini airfield. The first seven aircraft shipped up from the Union had SAAF Sky Blue lower surfaces, while the additional Fury Mk. Is assembled and received from Eastleight, had Black and White lower surfaces. The two different colour schemes can clearly be identified on the lower cowlings of these two Furies. Also of note is the additional panels fitted in front of the radiator on the right hand side ex-RAF Fury.

erts Heights. The six aircraft were camouflaged in Dark Green and Dark Earth upper surfaces, with SAAF Sky Blue lower surfaces. The light colour of the lower surface can clearly be discerned on photographs of some of these Furies. These photographs show the contrast between the light blue of the original Furies and the Black of the Black and White ex-RAF scheme very clear, especially on the lower cowlings. The Furies had Type A1 roundels applied to the fuselage sides in Orange, White, Blue and Yellow colours. The roundels above the upper wings appeared to be close proximity to the later Type C roundels in Orange, White and Blue colours (with a thin White circle separating the Orange and Blue circles), while Type A roundels in Orange, White and Blue were applied below the lower wings. Fin flashes of Orange, White and Blue were applied to the vertical fin, with the Orange leading on both sides. The serial numbers were applied to the rear fuselages in Black, and were 8 inches (203 mm) tall.

During September 1939, a number of the Furies of 43 Squadron (RAF) were camouflaged in Dark Green and Dark Earth upper surfaces, and the pattern used on the SAAF Furies seems to have followed the pattern of these Furies quite closely. Photographs show that there were also two patterns applied of which one was a mirror image of the other. The 43 Squadron Furies had

Hawker Fury 203 at Zwartkops Air Station, shortly after delivery in September 1936. The Fury is finished in silver doped fabric and polished natural metal sections. The serial number is applied only to the rear fuselage in Black. Type A roundels were painted in Orange/White/Blue on the rear fuselages, above the upper wing and below the lower wing. The Orange was in the centre of the roundels with the Blue being the outer circle.

The only photograph that the authors have ever seen showing the upper surfaces of a SAAF Fury in East Africa. The roundels above the upper wings are clearly visible and all three colours of Orange, White and Blue can be discerned in this photograph. The roundel almost appears to be a modified Type C roundel, with the fairly narrow White band between the Orange inner and Blue outer circles. The camouflage pattern on the upper wing is also visible in the photograph.

their lower fuselage surfaces and lower surfaces of the left hand upper and lower wings finished in Black, with the lower surfaces on the right hand upper and lower wings painted in White. The lower surfaces of both tailplanes were finished in Black. From available photographs, it can be seen that the ex-RAF Furies used by the SAAF in East Africa also carried this finish.

On completion of their service with 2 Squadron, the Furies were used, with Mohawks, by 4 Squadron for their training at 70 OTU.

Gloster Gauntlet and Gladiator

The SAAF pilots of 1 Squadron started their conversion training at Abu Sueir, Egypt on 29 May 1940. Initially they flew Gloster Gauntlets, while their Gloster Gladiators were being assembled from ex-RAF stocks. The first nine Gladiators left Egypt for East Africa on 24 July 1940 and arrived at Nairobi on 24 July 1940. A second batch of nine Gladiators left Abu Sueir on 7 August 1940, arriving at Khartoum on 8 August. This part of the squadron was then named as 1 Squadron, while the parent unit, crew and aircraft in Nairobi was renumbered to 2 Squadron. At the end of October 1940, the 2 Squadron Gladiators were withdrawn and sent to supplement those from 1 Squadron. The Gladiators were eventually transferred to 237 (Rhodesian) Squadron in February 1941.

2 Squadron received three Gloster Gauntlets in January 1941, but these aircraft were also in a bad state and one was immediately cannibalised to keep the other two flying. They were primarily used as escort for the General Officer Commanding's DH.89 Dragon Rapide when flying around in the East African Theatre.

After a number of Hawker Hurricane losses, 3 Squadron was also equipped with 12 Gladiators in April 1941. Nine aircraft came from 94 Squadron (RAF) and three from the Aden Station Flight. These aircraft were well used and visibly in a very weathered condition when received. The unit later re-equipped with the Mohawk IV, but the type had engine problems for its complete service period in the SAAF.

The initial batch of Gladiators received in Egypt were finished in the standard Temperate Land Scheme for fighter aircraft at the time as specified in the Air Directive 1162 "Camouflage Scheme for Single Engine Biplanes". Two pat-

Lt W. P. Stanford (left) and Lt R. K. Stevenson from 2 Squadron while on standby with their Hawker Furies at Vittoria. This was an ex-RAF Fury Mk. I and the split between the Black and White lower surfaces of the upper wing is clearly visible. Note the very weathered condition of the black paint on the radiator area of the aircraft, the paint on the landing gear strut and that on the fuselage side above the wing leading edge.

One of the last two Gauntlets operated by 2 Squadron photographed from a Junkers Ju 86 which it was escorting at the time. Note the SAAF Sky Blue lower surfaces and the Type A1 roundel applied to the fuselage sides. The Gauntlets had Type B roundels applied to the top surfaces of both upper wings, as can be seen in the photograph in the bottom.

terns, namely an A- and B-Scheme, were used, and the colours used were Dark Earth/Dark Green and Light Earth/Light Green upper surface camouflage, while the lower surfaces of the wings and fuselage were painted in White and Black colours. Typically the right hand lower surfaces were painted in White, while the left hand side were finished in Black. Both patterns have been identified on the Gladiators operated by the SAAF, with some also showing small variations in the official scheme patterns.

The principle of the upper surface camouflage was to paint the areas that would be cast in shadows a lighter colour than the remaining areas, in order to give the overall aircraft a uniform appearance. The Dark Green/Dark Earth camouflage finish was applied to the upper surfaces on the upper wings, the upper portions of the fuselage (typically from around mid-way) and the upper surfaces of the tailplane. The shadow areas on the upper surfaces of the lower wings, the vertical fin and rudder, the areas of the fuselage in the shadow of the upper wings and the lower fuselage, were then covered in the Light Earth/Light Green camouflage finish.

During the East African Campaign, the lower surfaces were repainted in a new colour called SAAF Sky Blue. The Gladiators were also re-painted as can be seen in some photographs of the type. The change was authorised by a Middle East Letter S.45273 dated 15 August 1940, calling for the colour Light (Middle East) Blue. The order mentioned that the lower surfaces at present painted in White and Black,

The last two Gauntlets operated by 2 Squadron photographed with the de Havilland Rapide of the General Officer Commanding whom they were escorting. Note the individual code letters which had now been applied to the Gauntlets. The photographer used an orthochromatic film, but it is believed that the code letters were in Orange, matching the shade in the fin flash and roundels.

A photograph of Gladiator Mk. II N5818 received by the SAAF in Abu Sueir. The four colours of the upper surface camouflage can clearly be seen in the photograph. Gladiator N5818 is finished in the B-scheme.

were in the process of being changed to Light (Middle East) Blue.

The Gladiators had Type A1 roundels applied to the fuselages. The SAAF replaced the Red in the RAF markings with Orange, i.e. the centre of the roundels and on the fin flash. This instruction was contained in a number of orders and instructions. These included the SAAF Aircraft Colour Orders for Camouflage and Markings in East Africa dated 17 September 1940, which stated that all SAAF aircraft had to carry Orange centres. Technical Order A125/gen 12 on Camouflage and Markings, dated December 1940, also repeated the aspect of Orange centres, as did the Minutes from the Director General Air Force 12/4/20/1 dated 20 January 1942, which again re-iterated Orange centres on all camouflaged SAAF aircraft. There were also references from Lewis and Berger, the main paint suppliers to the SAAF in East Africa to Orange paint stocks, including a tender No. B.129370 dated 1 January 1940 for Orange paint for the centre of the roundels. From these it can be seen, that the SAAF units would make every effort to comply with these instructions and orders, and paint the aircraft roundels under their control as required. Although aircraft might have retained the Red for a short period on arrival, it is clear from a number of War Diary entries across numerous units that every effort was made to repaint these as soon as practical after receipt of the aircraft.

The Gladiators had Type B roundels on the upper surfaces of both top wings, again with Orange centres. The left hand bottom wing had a Type A roundel applied (with the Yellow outline), in order to make the roundel more visible against the dark background. This prevented the Blue section from disappearing against the Black colour. From photographs, it appear that when the lower surfaces were re-painted in SAAF Sky Blue, no roundels were applied to the lower surfaces of the wings. The fin flashes were in Orange, White and Blue, with the Orange leading. Serial numbers were applied to the rear fuselage in Black. No unit emblems or individual code letters were applied to the 1 and 2 Squadron SAAF Gladiators.

Gloster Gladiator Mk. II N5822 was received during June 1940 from No. 6 Squadron RAF and was operated by 1 Squadron during the East African Campaign. The aircraft was shot down by a CR.42 near Aroma on 12 January 1941 and the pilot, Lt J. S. R. Warren, was killed in action.

Gladiator Mk. II N5815 was one of three Gladiators being transferred back to 1 Squadron when Gladiator N5813 was shot down on 9 November 1940. N5815 was used by 1 Squadron for training in Abu Sueir and later transferred to 2 Squadron for a short period, before being returned to 1 Squadron during October 1940. During early 1941, the Gladiator was again transferred to K Flight.

The SAAF received 18 Gladiators, which were flown down to Nairobi and Khartoum to equip 1 and 2 Squadrons. The four colours of the upper surface camouflage can clearly be seen in this photographs of the line-up of aircraft. Gladiator Mk. II N5818 leading the line-up and the second aircraft are both finished in the B-scheme, while the third aircraft is finished in the A-scheme. Note the Yellow surround to the roundel on the Black lower surfaces of the left hand bottom wing. Some of the aircraft also does not have the usual wheel disks fitted to the hubs.

The 3 Squadron Gladiators received from 94 Squadron and the Aden Flight, initially still carried the GO code of 94 Squadron applied to the fuselages in what appears to be a light grey colour, presumably Medium Sea Grey. The aircraft were in a very weathered state, but initial operational pressure prevented them from immediately being re-painted. They were also finished in the four primary colours on the upper surfaces, with Black and White lower surfaces. Some also had a rear fuselage band painted around the fuselage, in what appears to be standard RAF Sky. The fuselage roundels were also weathered on the aircraft and seems to have been a mix of Type A1 roundels and Type A roundels. The roundels still had the RAF Red centres. The left hand bottom wings also had the Type A1 roundels applied as on the other Gladiators operated by the SAAF. The fin flashes were, however, of a non-standard size, as they were very narrow compared to the standard for the period. They were in Red, White and Blue, with the Red leading. The serial numbers were applied in Black and were in a small and non-standard font on the rear fuselage.

The 3 Squadron Gladiators were eventually re-painted and then received new serial numbers in the SAAF serial system and the block of 1321 to

3 Squadron's Gladiators were repainted and the aircraft then received new serial numbers in the SAAF serial system. This photograph of Gladiator Mk. II 1339 shows the new simplified colour scheme of Dark Earth and Dark Green upper surfaces. The roundel is much smaller than previously and the fin flash lines are shorter than on other aircraft. The Gladiator has a name which seems to be "Pinky" painted on the rudder. The SAAF at one time fitted modified Savoia S.79 propellers to some of the Gladiators, as in this photograph.

1350 was allocated. A photograph shows Gladiator 1333 in the new simplified colour scheme of Dark Earth and Dark Green upper surfaces, in the same manner of the colour schemes of the single engine Hurricanes, Furies and Hartebeeste that the SAAF operated in East Africa. The newly applied roundels were smaller than those previously applied to the 1 and 2 Squadron Gladiators. It is very difficult to comment on the lower surfaces from this photograph, but it still seems to be very dark and possibly still in Black and White, as the roundel is still highly visible on the lower left hand wing and the inboard side of the right hand main gear leg is still a light shade. The SAAF orders at the time already called for Light Blue lower surfaces.

A photograph of Gladiator 1339 in the new simplified colour scheme of Dark Earth and Dark Green upper surfaces shows the roundel much smaller than previously and the tail flash lines are shorter than on Gladiator 1333. The lower surfaces of the aircraft still appear to be in a dark colour, such as the Black and White scheme. This Gladiator had a name which seems to be "Pinky" painted on the rudder. The actual name and colour is uncertain but is portrayed in Brown in a colour profile on page 70, to illustrate the position and tonal value.

Gladiator Mk. II, N2287/GO-E, serving with 3 Squadron, 1941. The Gladiator still carries the GO code of 94 Squadron and the individual code letter applied in front of the roundel. The aircraft were later over-painted and finally allocated SAAF serial numbers. Note the very weathered finish and freshly applied patches of paint. Only the white section of the fin flash had been applied. All these aircraft received by 3 Squadron had a very narrow fin flash applied to them.

Two Gloster Gladiators operated by 1 Squadron in East Africa, both in the prescribed colour scheme for single-engine biplanes of the period. The four different colours of Light and Dark Green and Light and Dark Earth used on the wing upper surfaces and fuselage sides of the scheme can clearly be made out on the closer aircraft.

The 1 Squadron pilots initially trained on Gauntlets at Abu Sueir in Egypt. From a period film taken by one of the squadron pilots with an 8 mm camera, it appears that these aircraft were finished in the Temperate Land Scheme, with Dark Earth and Dark Green upper surfaces. 2 Squadron later received three Gauntlets, which from photographs were also finished in the Temperate Land Scheme, with the lower surfaces finished in Sky Blue. These aircraft had Type A1 fuselage roundels applied, with Orange centres, Type B roundels on the upper surface of the top wing and Type A roundels on the lower surface of the bottom wings. The fin flashes were standard in Orange, White and Blue, with the Orange leading. SAAF serial numbers were applied in Black to the rear fuselages.

Two of the three aircraft were kept operational and they received the individual code letters of A and B applied to the rear fuselages. The photograph showing these codes was taken with an orthochromatic film, but it appears that the codes might have been applied in Orange paint, as they seems to be in the same colour as the roundel centres and forward section of the fin flash.

Hawker Hurricane Mk. I

In November 1936, The UK Air Ministry confirmed the sale of seven Hawker Hurricane Mk. Is to South Africa. The first three Hurricanes arrived by sea in Durban during February 1939. The packing crates were transported to the Stamford Hill airfield and the Hurricanes were then assembled by ground personnel

The Hawker Hurricane Mk. I was the newest fighter that the SAAF could field in limited numbers for most of the East African Campaign. Hurricane Mk. I L1708 arrived in South Africa during February 1939 and was assembled at Stamford Hill, Durban, where this photograph of it was taken. It was later re-serialled as 271.

Hurricane Mk. I L1710 was one of the first three Hurricanes delivered to South Africa. It is shown here being on arrival at Waterkloof Air Station, after the flight from Durban by Capt Preller on 7 March 1939. It was delivered finished in the standard RAF Dark Green and Dark Earth upper surfaces, with Aluminium painted lower surfaces. The orthochromatic film used by the photographer turned the yellow colour of the fuselage roundel to a dark colour.

which had been moved from Pretoria to Durban for the project. The aircraft were all fabric wing Mk. Is fitted with two-bladed propellers and Venturi inlets for the instrumentation. They had the normal short carburettor intake at the time of assembly.

After the assembly of the aircraft the Hurricanes were test flown on 6 March 1939, by Maj J. E. O. Marais, Maj S. A. Melville and Capt R. H. Preller. The first three Hurricanes that arrived were serial numbers L1708, L1710 and L1711. On 7 March, Capt Preller flew Hurricane L1710 to Waterkloof Air Station, in Pretoria. The time of 1 hour and 13 minutes was something never seen before in South Afica, who was very used to slow bi-planes taking much longer over the route and often with stops for refuelling in between.

The Hurricanes retained their RAF serial numbers until April 1939, when they were renumbered as follows: L1708 to 271, L1710 to 272 and L1711 to 273. By June 1939, a further three Hurricane Mk. Is had been delivered to Durban. These aircraft were also assembled and test Flown at Stamford Hill in Durban. They were serial numbers L1874, L1875 and L1876. These three aircraft were test flown by Capt Jack Mossop, who was the Officer Commanding of the Natal Air Training School and Capt St. Elmo "Saint" Truter of Pretoria, on 14 June 1939. These three aircraft were re-serialled as follows: L1874 to 274, L1875 to 275 and L1876 to 276. The seventh Hurricane of the original order, L1909, was delivered and assembled during September 1939. This aircraft was re-serialled as 277.

Hawker Hurricane Mk. I L1708 is seen here at Waterkloof Air Station during March 1939. It was one of the first four Hurricanes allocated to 1 Squadron when it was established for service in East Africa in 1940 and still had fabric wings and the original two-bladed propeller while serving in East Africa. The Hurricane was transferred to 2 Squadron and on 7 November 1940 was again transferred from 2 Squadron to 3 Squadron, which had arrived at Nairobi in October 1940.

Hawker Hurricane Mk. I, L1874 or L1876, seen here at Waterkloof Air Station after being delivered from Stamford Hill by Capt Jack Mossop. Note the B-scheme visible on the fuselage.

Hawker Hurricane Mk. I L1710 seen at Waterkloof Air Station during March 1939. The serial numbers below the wings were positioned to read from the leading edge on the right hand wing and from the trailing edge on the left hand wing. The big Type A roundels on the lower surfaces are visible as well.

Hawker Hurricane Mk. I L1711 seen at Waterkloof Air Station during April 1939. The aircraft is in the process of being re-serialled and the new serial number, 273, has already roughly been applied to the rear fuselage in white to indicate the final serial number allocated to the aircraft. The new serial number would finally be painted in 8-inch high numbers in Black.

The Type A1 roundels in Orange, White, Blue and Yellow rings are clearly visible on the upper wings and fuselage of the Hurricane being prepared for the test flight at Stamford Hill by Capt Jack Mossop, on 14 June 1939. This was one of the second batch of aircraft delivered to South Africa. The aircraft has the B-scheme applied and is thus either L1874 or L1876.

At the time of the delivery of the Hurricanes, the RAF aircraft camouflage schemes were based on two main paint schemes, namely the Temperate Land Scheme of Dark Green and Dark Earth upper surfaces and the Temperate Sea Scheme of Dark Slate Grey and Extra Dark Sea Grey upper surfaces. These were followed later by the addition on 15 August 1941, of the Day Fighter Scheme of Dark Green and Ocean Grey upper surfaces and on 22 August 1942 the Tropical or Desert Scheme of Dark Earth and Middle Stone upper surfaces.

On delivery in South Africa, the Hurricanes were finished in the Temperate Land Scheme of Dark Green and Dark Earth upper surfaces. The lower surfaces were in Aluminium. At the time various combinations of White and Black lower surfaces overall or in combination with the Aluminium were in use in England and on the aircraft deployed to France. On 6 June 1940, a new finish of Sky was introduced on all lower surfaces. This was followed by the new Day Fighter Scheme lower surface of Medium Sea Grey on 15 August 1941 and the Tropical Land Scheme with Azure Blue on 22 August 1942.

On delivery the Hurricanes carried Type A roundels of 45 inches (1143 mm) diameter below both main wings. These were positioned with their centres 57 inches (1448 mm) from the wing tip, and no part of the roundel touched the ailerons. The fuselage had Type A1 roundels applied of 35 inches (889 mm) diameter, while the upper wings had Type A1 roundels of 49 inches (1245 mm) diameter applied on both wings. In all cases the original RAF roundel centres were over-painted in Orange to indicate the SAAF ownership of the aircraft. The serial numbers were painted in 6 inches (152 mm) numbers in Black on the rear fuselages and were repeated below both main wings in 30 inches (762 mm) high numbers. These were placed to read from the leading edge on the right hand wing and from the trailing edge on the left hand wing. Initially no fin flashes were carried.

Initially the aircraft upper surfaces were finished in two p atterns, namely an A-scheme and

Hawker Hurricane Mk. I 272 (ex-L1710) seen serving with 1 Squadron at Port Reitz, Mombasa, Kenya. The new lower surface colour of SAAF Sky Blue can be seen, as well as the tropical filter which was added to protect the Rolls Royce Merlin engine from dust during operations. The Hurricane was finished in the B-scheme and had SAAF Type A1 roundels applied to the fuselage and SAAF Type A roundels applied to the lower wing surfaces. During these early months of the war, the upper wing roundels were modified Type B roundels with Yellow outer circles, later to be replaced by full Type B roundels with Orange centres.

Hurricane Mk. I 284 at Addis Ababa during 1941. The standard Type B upper wing roundels are clearly visible, as is the individual code letter, J, believed to be in a light grey colour. The Hurricane is finished in the A-scheme. This Hurricane was used by Lt Bob Kerhaw in the rescue of Capt Jack Frost.

Hurricane Mk. Is 279 (right) and 278 (below right) were allocated to 3 Squadron and were flown from Waterkloof Air Station to Nairobi in October 1940 by 2/Lt J. P. Upton and 2/Lt S. D. Marsh respectively. The aircraft had all-metal wings, three-bladed propellers and the newer version of the radio mast fitted to the top of the fuselages. The aircraft were finished in Dark Green and Dark Earth upper surfaces, with SAAF Sky Blue lower surfaces. The Type A1 fuselage roundels on Hurricane 278 were distinctly smaller than those applied to the remainder of the fleet. Both carried Type B roundels on the upper wings and Type A roundels on the lower wing surfaces. The fin flashes were in Orange, White and Blue, with the Orange leading on both sides. The serial numbers were in Black on the rear fuselage and during late November 1940 the "Fighting Wasp" unit insignia of 3 Squadron were added to both sides of the nose. Hurricane 279 had the code letter D applied to both sides of the rear fuselage in what appears to be fresh red paint or possibly orange paint.

[This page] Hurricane Mk. I 277 (ex-L1909) seen here at Port Reitz, Mombasa after delivery to 1 Squadron in 1940. The modified upper wing roundel can be seen in the enlargement in the left. Here it can be seen that the Orange and Blue had both been extended to cover the original white portion of the Type A1 roundel, but that the Yellow surrounding outer ring had been retained. These roundels were later replaced by standard Type B roundels containing only the Orange centres and Blue outer rings. Note the name "Goof" applied to both sides of the nose. This is the only SAAF aircraft that the authors have seen photographs of, with a name applied on it during the East African Campaign, although there are rumours of more aircraft with names applied to them.

B-scheme which were a mirror image of each other. On Hurricanes, the A-scheme was usually applied to aircraft with a serial number ending on an odd number and the B-scheme to those ending on an even number, but exceptions did exist. The A-scheme can be seen on the available photographs of Hurricane L1711 and the B-scheme on those of L1710. This practise was later discontinued and most aircraft finished only in one of the patterns.

At the outbreak of W.W. II, the Hurricanes were initially transferred to Cape Town to serve as part of the Coastal Defence Unit. They were operated by 6 Squadron, based at the Cape Air Training School at Youngsfield. Of the five aircraft that left Waterkloof Air Station for Cape Town in September 1939, only three remained in a serviceable state, namely 271, 273 and 274. Hurricane 272 nosed over during take off at Beaufort West after hitting a soft sandy patch and 275 was destroyed in a crash while attempting a downwind landing at Youngsfield by 2/Lt Derrick Tyler. He experienced an engine failure as the aircraft arrived overhead the airfield. He was sadly killed in the accident. Hurricane 276 had earlier been destroyed in a crash at Zwartkops Air Station on 12 June 1939 and was later allocated to units in East Africa to be used as spare parts to keep the remainder of the aircraft operational.

The three remaining aircraft experienced engine problems due to operating off the dusty inland airfields without proper air filters. The engines were removed and sent up to the Air Depot for overhauling. Thus all three Hurricanes remained in Cape Town without engines. During May 1940 they were railed up to Pretoria where they received overhauled engines and were delivered to the new 1 Squadron being established at Waterkloof Air Station. They were joined by 277, which now served as the fourth aircraft on the squadron. On 22 May 1940, the Hurricanes were flown to Kenya by the pilots of 1 Squadron, for operations against the Italian

Hurricane Mk. I 285 being run up at Waterkloof Air Station before departing to East Africa in October 1940. The tropical filter has already been fitted and the aircraft lower surfaces are already painted in SAAF Sky Blue. The spinner is finished in Black and fin flashes covered the complete fin area. The Hurricane was flown to Nairobi in East Africa by Major L. A. "Larry" Wilmot, the Officer Commanding, 3 Squadron.

Forces in East Africa. The unit also had some Hawker Furies, which were shipped from Durban to East Africa.

By now, the Hurricanes had tropical air filters fitted to them to prevent the previous engine problems and they had received a change in their colour schemes. The lower surfaces were now painted in a new colour, called SAAF Sky Blue, and the aircraft also had fin flashes applied of Orange, White and Blue, with the Orange leading on both sides. The fin flashes on these seven aircraft varied in width from available photographs of two of the aircraft. Hurricane 272 had the complete fin covered with the three colour bands being of equal width, while Hurricane 277 had three bands of 9 inches (229 mm) each with the forward section of the fin in the standard camouflage colour. In later aircraft the fin flashes consisted of the Blue and White bands in 9 inches (229 mm) bands, with the Orange covering the rest of the vertical fin area as seen on Hurricanes 278 and 279. The upper wing roundels were initially modified by painting out the White circle with Orange and Blue, but were later replaced by standard Type B roundels containing only Orange centres with Blue outer rings.

The Hurricanes and Furies that were operated by 1 Squadron, were all transferred to 2 Squadron, when the part of the unit operating from Nairobi was renamed to 2 Squadron on 1 October 1940. The Flight operating Gloster Gladiators from Khartoum for the defence of the Sudan, retained the title 1 Squadron and received more Gladiators to build up their aircraft numbers. The lower serial numbered Hurricanes were thus now operated by 2 Squadron.

The initial seven Hurricanes were supplemented by nine more that arrived in South Africa on 12 September 1939, on board the ship "Rochester Castle". The aircraft were offloaded in the Cape Town harbour and were moved by road to Wingfield. Here the Hurricanes were assembled by the newly formed No. 9 Air Depot. These aircraft were late Hurricane Mk. Is fitted with the all-metal wings instead of the fabric covered wings of the previous seven aircraft. They also had three-bladed propellers in place of the original two-bladed versions still fitted to the older models. The first one of this batch of Hurricanes was ready for test flying on 20 September 1940. After the test flights were concluded the aircraft were all flown up to Waterkloof Air Station where the first eight arrived on 2 October, with the last one arriving on 6 October 1940. These Hurricanes received the serial numbers 278 up to and including 286. The nine aircraft were allocated to the newly formed 3 Squadron for operations in East Africa. The unit departed Waterkloof Air Station on 16 October and eight aircraft arrived safe at Nairobi on 22 October 1940.

One of the aircraft, 283, was damaged during the transit when it crashed at Mpika after 2/Lt H. M. Torr returned to the airfield due to bad weather en-route. The Hurricane was later repaired by a team from No. 6 Air Depot at Eastleigh and was ferried to Nairobi on 13 November 1940 by Capt S. V. Theron.

Soon after the arrival of 3 Squadron at Nairobi, on 25 October, the unit received six additional Hawker Hurricane Mk. Is which were assembled at Eastleigh. These were all late Hurricane Mk. Is with metal wings and three-bladed propellers, and carried the serial numbers 287 (V7280), 289 (P3253), 290 (V7281), 291 (P3257), 293 (P3262) and 294 (P3252).

Although the ex-RAF Gladiators and Furies received by 1 and 2 Squadron respectively were finished in White (right hand side) and Black (left hand side) lower surfaces, the Hurricane lower surfaces were finished in SAAF Sky Blue. This was in accordance with Letter S.45273 issued by the Headquarters Middle East on 15 August 1940, where it stated that the Hurricanes were to be finished in Light (Middle East) Blue.

The Hurricanes were finished in Dark Green and Dark Earth upper surfaces and both the A- and B-schemes were still present on the aircraft. This can be seen by the B-scheme applied to Hurricane 278 and the A-scheme applied to Hurricane 279. The fin flashes on these aircraft consisted of 9 inches (229 mm) wide Blue and White bands, with the Orange covering the rest of the vertical tailfin area above the tailplanes.

Later during the campaign some of the Hurricanes received individual code letters which were applied to the rear fuselage on both sides. Although it cannot be stated with total certainty, studies from photographs that were taken with normal and orthochromatic film, seem to indicate that these code letters were painted in a light grey colour. There is one aircraft, however, namely 289 flown by Capt Jack Frost, which seems to have the code letter applied in Yellow. As he was a Flight Commander with 3 Squadron at the time, it is quite plausible that his aircraft code letter was painted in a different colour, as a study of the unit emblem on his aircraft, also shows that to be in different colours compared to the remainder of the squadron's aircraft. One other aircraft, 279/D, seems to have had the code letter painted in Orange or Red. The available photograph is taken with an orthochromatic film, as can be seen by the dark shades of the orange and yellow in the roundels and fin flash, with the code letter being even darker than the black serial number, thus indicating a colour shade reversed by the film, such as fresh orange or red. A later photograph shows the code letter to be re-painted in the same light grey shade as the majority of the Hurricanes.

During December 1940, 2 Squadron returned their Hurricanes to 1 Squadron and received additional Furies, and on 4 January 1941 they operated twelve Furies and three Gauntlets. At the Port Sudan Detachment of 1 Squadron, the following Hurricane serial numbers were recorded during December 1940; 272, 273, 274, 285, 288, and 297. Capt Driver serving here damaged a Savoia S.79 flying 274 on 9 December, and again damaged two S.79s on 16 December 1940 flying 285. Hurricane 273 was damaged in a crash on landing on 16 December, while being flown by Lt Taylor.

Some of the Hurricanes from 3 Squadron also returned to 1 Squadron, for example 291 serving with the Oxo Detachment during January and February 1941. Hurricane 298 was also recorded serving with 1 Squadron during this period, but was in turn again allocated to 3 Squadron and served with this unit on 29 March 1941, when Lt Bob Kershaw operated it on standby duties. During March 1941, Hurricane 299 was recorded with the HQ-Flight of 3 Squadron operating at Jiggiga. This was the highest serial recorded for the Hurricane Mk. Is operated by the SAAF during the East African Campaign.

A later photograph of Hurricane Mk. I 279 now showing the code letter to be painted in the same light grey shade as the majority of the remainder of the Hurricanes. This photograph was taken at Garissa towards the end of 1940.

Hurricane Mk. IIB, HV509/K, of 41 Squadron. Note the Bristol Beaufort and Martin Baltimore in the background of the photograph. The third aircraft could be a Bristol Blenheim Mk. V. Both Hurricanes have long range tanks below the wings and are being refuelled for a next mission. The spinner on Hurricane K is in Sky, while that of the second Hurricane appear to be Black. Hurricane HV509 and HV480 were the third Flight to route from Gilgil to Mombasa in December 1942 and this photograph could show these two aircraft soon after arrival in Mombasa.

During the final stages of the Campaign the Hurricanes appeared very weathered with faded and patched paintwork. The Dark Green and Dark Earth upper surfaces were retained, with the SAAF Sky Blue lower surfaces. The roundels were standardised with SAAF Type A1 on the fuselages, Type B on the upper wings and Type A on the lower surfaces, all with Orange centres. Fin flashes consisted of 9 in (229 mm) Blue and White bands with the remainder of the forward section of the fin in Orange. Serial numbers and spinners were finished in Black and some aircraft carried individual codes, believed to have mainly been in a light grey colour.

Hawker Hurricane Mk. IIB

One other unit, namely 41 Squadron, would exchange their Hawker Hartebeeste for a new batch of Hurricanes, operating as a holding force after the Campaign was over. On 25 May 1942, while based at Nairobi, the Officer Commanding was informed that the proposed reorganisation of the squadron to a Fighter Squadron, had been agreed to. The Squadron would receive 16 Hawker Hurricanes to arm two Flights. In the interim a Hartebeest Flight with nine aircraft was to be maintained by the squadron.

On the afternoon of 23 October, five Hurricanes and a Blenheim arrived at Gilgil, under command of Capt Alexander and 41 Squadron finally became a full Fighter Squadron. Another five Hurricanes arrived on the morning of 24 October, with two Hurricanes departing for Eastleigh in the afternoon to have the long range tanks removed. During the landing at Eastleigh on the morning of 25 October, one aircraft, HV486, was badly damaged on landing. On inspection of the new Hurricanes, it was found that the tyres were badly worn, most likely as a result of using a tar-runway at their previous base. The next day two more Hurricanes departed to Eastleigh to have the long range tanks removed. Four more left and returned from Eastleigh on 29 October, for the removal of

The 41 Squadron Hawker Hurricane Mk. IIBs on their arrival at Gilgal, during the last week of October 1942. The photograph shows the right hand side of the HV490/X fitted with the long range tanks, with HV515/J visible second in the line up. Note the rough and different application of the distemper paint.

Hurricane Mk. IIB HV515/J leads the line up of Hurricanes of 41 Squadron, shortly after their arrival at Gilgil. The Hurricanes were ferried across Africa from Takoradi on the West Coast, assisted by a Blenheim serving as navigation lead aircraft. The Hurricanes still have the white ferry markings applied to them to assist in search and rescue, should they go down somewhere along the route. The Hurricanes carry the standard markings as per orders for the 1942 era, namely Type C1 fuselage roundels, Type C under-wing roundels and Type B upper wing roundels, all with Orange centres to indicate the SAAF owner-ship. The fin flashes were 24x24 inch and propeller spinners were finished in different colours.

the tanks. On 30 October, one aircraft, HV480, made a safe landing when the canopy hood had been torn off during flight, damaging the empennage in the process.

The exterior finish of the Hurricane Mk. IIBs as received by 41 Squadron followed the typical RAF orders for the 1942 period and the aircraft were finished in the Temperate Land Scheme. The upper surfaces of the Hurricanes were in Dark Green and Dark Earth camouflage, with the lower surfaces in Sky. The aircraft carried 36 inches (914 mm) Type C1 roundels on the fuselage and the fin flashes on the aircraft were 24 x 24 inches (610 x 610 mm), with the Orange and Blue bands being 11 inches (279 mm) wide each and the White band being 2 inches (51 mm) wide. The upper wings had 49 inches (1245 mm) Type B roundels applied while the lower wings had 32 inches (813 mm) Type C roundels applied. The aircraft carried the serial number in 8 inches (203 mm) high Black numbers on the rear fuselage. The aircraft had individual code letters applied to the rear fuselages in what appear to be White. On arrival at

Hurricane Mk. IIB HV500/Q on stand-by with the pilot and crew relaxing in the shaded of a tree. The Hurricane is finished in Dark Green/Dark Earth upper surfaces in the A-scheme, with Sky lower surfaces. The aircraft carries the standard markings as per orders for the 1942 era with Type C1 fuselage roundels, Type C under-wing roundels and Type B upper wing roundels, all with Orange centres to indicate the SAAF owner-ship. The code letter appears to be in White, with the spinner in Red.

Mohawk Mk. IV 2529 taxiing out for another flight. The Type B upper wing roundels can be seen, as well as the Type A1 fuselage roundels.

Gilgil, the Hurricanes still had their long range tanks under the wings, as well as the White distemper ferry markings on the upper surfaces of the tailplanes and rear fuselage. These were removed in squadron service, as discussed in the text. The spinners seem too have had a mix of finishes and it appear that Red, Black and Sky spinners can be identified in one photograph of three aircraft on the line. On some aircraft the serial number or individual code was also applied to the drop tanks in what appear to be a white finish, most likely the same distemper used for the search and rescue markings.

41 Squadron arrived in North Africa on 6 May 1943 and started training on Hurricane Mk. IIBs. On 12 May 1943, the Squadron found itself at Shandur where they were being stationed, with one Flight deployed to Hughada and another to Agaba in Transjordan. Thus ended the SAAF use of Hurricanes in East Africa, although the Hurricane would still shoulder on with the SAAF in the Middle East and Desert Campaigns, as well as in the Union with 11 Operational Training Unit.

Curtiss Mohawk Mk. IV

The SAAF received 72 Mohawk IV aircraft. Most were delivered by sea from the United Kingdom, with spare parts also being supplied by ship from North America. The SAAF Representative in Washington, Col Holthouse, reported on 28 February that he could give no further information regarding any despatch of the aircraft, as it would depend entirely on when British ships would be available. The first Mohawk, with British serial number AR636, was shipped to Takoradi on the Gold Coast. The aircraft made its first flight on 22 December 1940, crashing into the sea minutes later due to a seized engine. Major modifications were required to the engines. These engine problems were to plague the Mohawks for their entire service career in the SAAF. The first nine aircraft sent to Mombasa with the intention to re-equip 3 Squadron during March 1941, all had un-modified engines. These engines had to be returned to Britain for modifications.

On 13 July 1941, it was reported that although the majority of Mohawks allocated for South Africa and the Middle East were awaiting shipment in the United Kingdom, 20 Mohawks were already at Mombasa, of which four of these aircraft had modified engines. The modified engines for the rest were at sea. Before being issued to 3 Squadron, some of the aircraft in East Africa were used by 4 Squadron, who was training on the type at 70 Operational Training Unit, Nakuru, Kenya (70 OTU). The unit

[Bottom] This photograph of Mohawk Mk. IV 2515 shows the large underwing roundel that the aircraft were delivered with. On the re-painted aircraft, it seems that a smaller version of the Type A roundel was usually applied. Another feature of re-painted aircraft was that the demarcation line of the upper and lower surface colours on re-painted aircraft was along the centre of the leading edge, while the original demarcation line was below the leading edges of the wings.

[Bottom right] Mohawk Mk. IV 2516/D in a typical setting with the ground crew working on the engine of the aircraft. The Mohawk was plagued by engine problems throughout the type's career in the SAAF. The code letter D appears to be applied in white paint. The new SAAF serial number was applied over the individual code letter in black paint.

Another Mohawk showing the Type B roundels applied to the upper wing surfaces. The centre was Orange with a Blue outer ring. The camouflage pattern can be seen on the left hand wing.

trained in East Africa between April 1941 and September 1941. During July, the squadron moved from Nakuru to Nanyuki, with six Mohawks and two Audax.

One of the problems associated with the move was whether the Mohawks were to be fitted with bomb racks and if so, what additions would be necessary before sending them to the Middle East, as was the intention at the time. On 28 July, it was further reported that ten modified engines had arrived and were being installed, that six aircraft with modified engines were in the process of being assembled and further, that 4 Squadron with the bulk of its transport and 16 aircraft would be ready for the move up North in a fortnight.

The Command in East Africa was at the time still uncertain as to how many aircraft 4 Squadron were to be given. The problem was solved at the end of the month, when Air Head Quarters, East Africa (A.H.Q.E.A.), was instructed to go ahead with the operational training on Mohawks and bring the squadron up to full equipment and personnel strength. When ready, the squadron were to leave Egypt without their Mohawks, which were to be allocated to 70 OTU. In addition it was reported that a further five Mohawks were on their way to Mombasa. The Head Quarters RAF Middle East (H.Q.R.A.F.M.E.) would inform A.H.Q.E.A. when they were ready to receive 4 Squadron and would hopefully on their arrival, equip the unit with Tomahawks.

On 4 August 1941 the A.H.Q.E.A. reported in its daily Mayfly that 4 Squadron had three and Eastleigh 19 Mohawks on the day. On 7 August it was reported that ten Mohawks had arrived in the S.S. "Belle Pareil" on 29 July and that six more Mohawks had arrived in the S.S. "Afrika" on 30 July at Mombasa. A further six Mohawks was expected to be on the S.S. "Floristan", which had not been unloaded yet. These were all direct consignments from the United Kingdom.

On 15 August, the Air Ministry at Kingsway sent a message to both H.Q.R.A.F.M.E. and A.H.Q.E.A. regarding the Mohawks spares in the Middle East, Takoradi and East Africa. The spares in East Africa were to be retained by the SAAF, while H.Q.M.E. were to send sufficient spares and ground equipment to Portugal when the opportunity arrived, to maintain 16 aircraft for four months. Spares and equipment at Takoradi could also be used towards this commitment. All remaining spares thereafter in the Middle East, had to be sent to India as soon as possible, where three Mohawk squadrons were to be formed. By 22 August, A.H.Q.E.A. reported that 21modified Mohawks were in operation, seven still had to be modified and 16 were still in cases and had to be assembled.

3 Squadron was eventually withdrawn to Nanyuki on 27 August 1941 for refit and training with the Mohawks, previously used by 4 Squadron. Three of these aircraft were attached to 41 Squadron and as 41 Squadron Detached Fighter Flight, were sent from Nairobi to the Vichy French border at Aiscia. Their primary target was a Savoia S.75, which was staging back and forth through Djibouti, bringing war material to the Italians.

During this month the unit was re-designated 3 Squadron, B-Flight. On 3 November 1941 the squadron had ten Mohawks available with A-Flight, while another five were serving with B-Flight. From November 1941 onwards, the Mohawks served mainly as ground attack aircraft, due to very limited Italian air opposition encountered. The final Mohawk operations against the Italian forces in East Africa, were flown on 27 November 1941. On this date eight Mohawks and 16 Hartebeeste took part in the final attacks on Gondor. By December most of 3 Squadron was back at Nairobi, with B-Flight still serving at Aiscia. Shortly hereafter, the Mohawks were returned to the Union, to be used

Mohawk IV 2509 forms the backdrop for this group of pilots photographed at Addis Ababa, late in 1941. The pilots were the aircrew from 3 Squadron, operating on the Mohawks, including some members from 4 Squadron who were detached to the unit at the time. The signboard carried the 3 Squadron emblem of the "Fighting Wasp".

as training aircraft by 5 and 7 Squadrons which were being formed and worked up.

By October 1941, 5 Squadron was working up on Mohawks at Germiston, also becoming operational on Tomahawks in the Middle East. On 15 January 1942, 7 Squadron had started training on the Mohawks at Zwartkops Air Station, in turn handing the aircraft over to 6 Squadron, on 2 April 1942. This squadron was activated on 23 February 1942, for home defence duties. The unit trained at Zwartkops Air Station and Durban, and subsequently operated mainly from Groutville, near Durban, and later from Eerste Rivier in Cape Town. The unit was disbanded during July 1943, when the threat of a Japanese invasion appeared to have passed.

A second unit for home defence, 10 Squadron, also formed during April 1942. It received its first four Mohawks from 6 Squadron on 26 May 1942. These were supplemented by Kittyhawk Mk. Is, operating from Durban. The first Kittyhawks were received on 28 June 1942, and by 1 August 1942, all the Mohawks had been returned to 6 Squadron. The unit was disbanded on 28 July 1943, and became B-Flight of 11 Operational Training Unit (11 OTU). 10 Squadron was reactivated at Almaza on 25 May 1944, and equipped with Spitfire Mk. Vs.

The Mohawks were delivered in Dark Green and Dark Earth upper surfaces, with Sky under surfaces. It is the author's opinion that some aircraft could still have carried the RAF equivalent Du Pont colours as finished in America, while some were over-painted in the actual RAF colours while in storage in the United Kingdom. The RAF serial numbers were replaced by SAAF serial numbers in the range 2501 to 2600 and the areas of the over-painted RAF serial numbers are visible in some of the Mohawk photographs. Roundels initially comprised of standard Type A on the fuselage and large under wing roundels, with Type B upper wing roundels. The fin flashes measured 24 x 27 inches (610 x 686 mm). The aircraft under surfaces were later repainted in SAAF Sky Blue and smaller Type A under wing roundels were painted on the wings. At least two aircraft had the right hand lower surfaces of the main wings and tail planes painted in Black, as well as the right hand lower half of the fuselage. Orange replaced the RAF Red on all roundels and fin flashes. Propeller

Mohawk Mk. IV 2506, previously BS784 in RAF service, is seen here after a landing accident where the aircraft tipped forward onto the propeller. The standard Type A1 roundel on the fuselage can be seen, as well as the position of the serial number, painted in Black. The fin flash consisted of Orange, White and Blue bars (Orange leading), while the upper wing roundels were Type B roundels.

spinners were observed in Natural Metal, Red and either Blue or Black.

Unit markings

The only SAAF fighter unit during the East African Campaign to have a squadron emblem painted on their aircraft, was 3 Squadron. The emblem first appeared on the Hawker Hurricanes that were operated by the squadron and again in a slightly modified version on their Mohawk IV fighters. The squadron's famous crest the "Fighting Wasp" with the motto "Semper Pugnans" translating to "Always Fighting" was adopted on 1 December 1940 with Maj Niblock-Stuart, previously the Officer Commanding 1 Squadron, taking over Command of the squadron on the same day. The design for the crest was taken from an American paper and improved upon by Mr R. C. Neill of Parkhurst, Johannesburg. The crest was also immediately applied to both sides of the nose on all the squadron's Hurricanes.

It is believed that the original design from which Mr. Neill worked, belonged to a US Navy Fighter Squadron VF-7. They were established on the 1 July 1939, and operated until 19 November 1940, under the name of "Blue Burglar Wasps". From June 1940 they operated from the aircraft carrier, USS "Wasp". On 19 November 1940, they were renumbered to VF-72, and became the "Fighting Wasps". VF-72 was disbanded on 29 March 1943. In the 3 Squadron badge, it would also appear that the wasp's body is possibly yellow and that the hat, eye, gloves and motto are a lighter colour, possibly white.

One of the most well-known SAAF aces and 3 Squadron Flight Commander, Capt Jack Frost, seems to have carried a modified version of this emblem on his aircraft. It also appears that his aircraft had the individual code applied in a

Members of 3 Squadron, clustered around the nose of the Hurricane Mk. I flown by Capt Jack Frost. He is standing third from the left. Fourth from the left, next to Capt Frost, is the Officer Commanding 3 Squadron, Maj J. D. Pretorius. A study of this photograph will also show the different colours used on the unit emblem, as applied to the Hurricane of Capt Frost, versus the standard colours used on the remaining squadron aircraft.

Captain Jack Frost, a 3 Squadron Flight Commander and ace pilot, seen climbing into his personal Hurricane Mk. I 289/M, which he operated until the end of his tour in East Africa. Although a section of the emblem is in the shade of the exhaust, enough of it is in good light conditions to see the differences when compared with the standard emblem.

Hurricane Mk. I 289/A was flown by Capt Frost as his last personal aircraft, before his departure back to the Union on 19 May 1941. On 17 July 1941, a new pilot, 2/Lt Lilienfield, carried out circuit practise in the aircraft, with the results as viewed. The Hurricane was finished in the standard SAAF colours of Dark Green and Dark Earth upper surfaces and SAAF Sky Blue lower surfaces. By now, the unique squadron emblem as carried by Capt Frost had been replaced with the standard version and the code letter A had been repainted in Light Grey. Standard roundels and fin flashes were applied for the period, with Black serial numbers.

A Hawker Hurricane Mk. I with the 3 Squadron "Fighting Wasp" emblem painted on the cowling. The emblem was typically painted on both sides of the engine, with the wasp facing forward on both sides.

[Far left] An enlarged version of the 3 Squadron emblem as applied to the Hurricanes operated by the squadron. The authors have interpreted the colours as follows: the wasp is depicted in yellow, with the boxing gloves, motto and hat in white; the background is a black circle.
[Left] A photograph of the modified version of the 3 Squadron "Fighting Wasp" emblem as applied to the Mohawk IVs operated by the squadron. The emblem appear to be in black, on a light blue background. The background could possibly be the same SAAF Sky Blue colour as used when re-painting the lower surfaces of the Mohawks.

Another photograph of the modified version of the 3 Squadron "Fighting Wasp" emblem as applied to the Mohawk IVs operated by the squadron. The emblem appear to be in a dark green stencil format, on a yellow background. This variation of the emblem, in the same colours as decribed here, was also applied to the post-war Harvards operated by 3 Squadron.

Mohawk Mk. IV 2537 leads a line-up of 3 Squadron Mohawks in East Africa. The unit emblem was applied to both sides of the nose on a light circular background, compared to the black painted background as found on the Hurricanes, previously operated by the squadron.

different colour to indicate his status as Flight Commander. From a clear photograph, it seems that the body of the wasp is painted in white with the boxing gloves and hat in red, while the wings remained in the original yellow colour presumed for the original emblem. It also appears that his Hurricane, 289, had the code letter applied in Yellow, instead of the light grey of the remaining Hurricanes.

The 3 Squadron "Fighting Wasp" emblem was also applied to both sides of some of the Mohawk IVs operated by the squadron. The emblem was, however, a modified version of that as seen on the Hurricanes. From available photographs, it appear that the background circle was changed to a light colour, presumed to be yellow. It also appear that the colours of the emblem was changed to a dark green stencil-format version of the previous emblem. This version of the emblem, in the described colours, were also applied post-war to the Harvards operated by 3 Squadron. Some aircraft also carried code letters on the rear fuselages, these appear to be mainly painted in Light Grey or White. A few aircraft were also observed with individual names painted on the fuselage sides, below the windshield. Unfortunately these names cannot be deciphered from the photos available to the author.

Presentation aircraft

Three aircraft, namely one Hawker Hurricane Mk. I and two Mohawk Mk. IVs, are known to have been presentation aircraft. This implied

A Hawker Hurricane Mk. I serving with 3 Squadron had the presentation or subscription name "South West Africa" applied to the fuselage. This indicated that the communities in the region, today known as Namibia, had contributed to the acquisition of the Hurricane. Unfortunately, the serial number is unknown.

that the community in a specific area would contribute funds towards the payment for an aircraft. Once allocated, the name of the area would be painted on the specific aircraft to indicate that the community had contributed towards the cost there-off.

There was only one Hurricane in East Africa, that the author is aware of, that carried a presentation title. The Hurricane Mk. I had the title "South West Africa" painted on the aircraft. The Hurricane was one of the second batch to have been delivered to South Africa and was flown to East Africa by 3 Squadron when they deployed to East Africa. The name was painted to both cockpit sides in black. South West Africa is today known as the independent country, Namibia. The individual serial number of the Hurricane could not be established, but the unit war Diary recorded that the aircraft was photographed on 15 October 1940.

Two Mohawks carried presentation titles, namely aircraft 2501 and 2511. Mohawk 2501 had the title "Die Waterberg" applied to it, while 2511 was named "Northern Transvaal". The Waterberg was the geographical mountaineous area to the north-west and north-east of Pretoria, bordered by the Springbok Flats, Warmbaths and Pietersburg, The Northern Transvaal was the area stretching north from Louis Trichardt, just south of the Soutpansberg mountains, across to the town of Messina and the northern border of the Union. Both of these communities were mainly farming areas in the Transvaal Province. The names were applied in black paint on both sides of the aircraft, with 2511 applied below the cockpit and 2501, more forward below the windshield.

[This page] **The two presentation Mohawk Mk. IVs operated by the SAAF. Mohawk 2501 was named "Die Waterberg" while Mohawk 2511 was named "Northern Transvaal". The pilot with 2501 is Capt Snowy Moody of 4 Squadron and that of 2511 is Lt H. E. N. Wildsmith, also of 4 Squadron.**

Color Plates

All color plates in this book (except the front cover) are reproduced to 1/48th scale

Gloster Gauntlet Mk. II, 871/A, 2 Squadron, 1940. The 1 Squadron pilots used a few Gauntlets during their conversion training at Abu Sueir, while 2 Squadron operated three Gauntlets, 870, 871 and 872, in East Africa. One was received in such a bad state that it was reduced to spares to keep the other two airworthy. The Gauntlets were operated by 2 Squadron until their move to Egypt in April 1941. They were usually flown as escorts for the Governor General's aircraft when he visited the area. By then the Gauntlets were finished in Dark Green and Dark Earth upper surfaces, with SAAF Sky Blue lower surfaces. They had standard SAAF Type B roundels applied to both upper wing top surfaces and SAAF Type A roundels applied to the lower wing bottom surfaces, with SAAF Type A1 roundels applied to the fuselage. The fin flashes were Orange, White and Blue with Black serial numbers on the rear fuselage. Two aircraft carried code letters A and B in what is presumed to be Orange paint. The serial tie-up is not known.

Gloster Gladiator Mk. II, N5851, 1940. N5851 had the lower surfaces of the fuselage and tailplanes repainted in SAAF Sky Blue, while the lower surfaces of the bottom wings were still in White (right) and Black (left) paint. The lower surface of the left wing had a SAAF Type A1 roundel applied, with a thin Yellow outer ring, to enhance the visibility of the Blue section of the roundel. The fuselage had a standard SAAF Type A1 roundel applied, and the top wings had SAAF Type B roundels applied to the upper surfaces. The fin flash was Orange, White and Blue. The aircraft served with 2 Squadron's C-Detachment during October 1940. It was one of the three Gladiators being transferred over to 1 Squadron when Gladiator N5813 was shot down on 8 November 1940. At 1 Squadron, the aircraft served with the Azaza Detachment during December 1940, where it was crashed by Lt Jarvis on 14 December. He was uninjured and camouflaged the Gladiator, until a salvage party could fetch it. It was later transferred to 6 Squadron RAF. On 26 September 1941, Sgt R. Walter from 6 Squadron RAF claimed one Savoia S.81 while flying N5851. This was the last biplane claim by the RAF.

Hawker Fury Mk. I, 208 (K5670), 1 Squadron, August 1940. Exterior finish consisted of Dark Earth and Dark Green upper surfaces, while the lower surfaces were finished in White on the right hand side and Black on the left hand side, split down the fuselage centre line. National markings consisted of SAAF A1 Type roundels applied to the fuselage sides and lower surfaces of both wings, with SAAF B Type roundels on the upper surfaces of the top wings. Fin flashes covered both sides of the vertical fin, although the width of the bars were non-standard. Individual aircraft markings consisted of the serial numbers in black on the rear fuselage. During August 1940, six additional Hawker Fury Mk. Is were assembled at Eastleigh, Nairobi and allocated to 1 Squadron. When the unit was renumbered to 2 Squadron on 1 October 1940, the Fury moved onto the strength of 2 Squadron and was reported with the B-Flight Detachment at Vittoria on 7 March 1941. The aircraft survived the East African Campaign and served in the SAAF until it crashed while operating with 43 Squadron from their base at Cato Ridge, near Durban, on 6 July 1942. The pilot, 2/Lt M. J. Krugel, was killed in the accident. At the time the aircraft carried the individual code letter X painted in white on the rear fuselage, while it was also coded S for a short period earlier in this squadron's service.

Gloster Gladiator Mk. II, N2289/GO-A. Operated by 3 Squadron during the East African Campaign. The unit received nine Gladiators from 94 Squadron RAF on 18 April 1941 and this aircraft still carries the GO squadron code of this unit. The Gladiators received from 94 Squadron were all numbered in the N22xx series. The Gladiator is finished in four colours of the Temperate Land Scheme for biplanes (Dark Earth/Dark Green and Light Earth/Light Green), but is heavily weathered. The lower left surface areas are finished in Black, while the right hand side lower surfaces are in White. The individual and unit code letters are in a Light Grey colour, while the serial numbers on these aircraft were in a small non-standard font in Black paint on the rear fuselages. The roundels still had the RAF Red centres when received. The fuselage carried Type A1 roundels, as well as the lower left hand wing, while the lower right hand wing carried a Type A roundel. The top surfaces of the upper wings had Type B roundels applied to them. The Gladiator has a tail band around the rear fuselage, in what is believed to be standard RAF Sky. The fin flash, in Red, White and Blue on this aircraft, was in a different size, compared to all the other received at the same time, with much wider bands covering the complete tailfin. The tailfin also had the non standard pattern seen on a number of these aircraft.

Gloster Gladiator Mk. II, 1339, 3 Squadron, 1941. The 3 Squadron Gladiators were eventually repainted and then received new serial numbers in the SAAF serial system. This is Gladiator 1339 in the new simplified colour scheme of Dark Earth and Dark Green upper surfaces. The roundel is much smaller than previously and the tail flash lines are shorter. The lower surfaces of the aircraft still appear to be in a dark colour, such as the Black and White scheme. The Gladiator has a name which seems to be "Pinky", painted on the rudder. The actual name and colour is uncertain but is portrayed in brown to illustrate the position and tonal value. The SAAF at one time struggled to get replacement propellers and then fitted modified Savoia S.79 propellers, which had been shortened, to some of the Gladiators like this one.

Gloster Gladiator Mk. II, N2287/GO-E. 3 Squadron was reinforced with nine Gladiators from 94 Squadron RAF and three Gladiators from the Aden Station Flight. Gladiator N2287 still carries the GO squadron identification code of 94 Squadron and the individual code letter applied in front of the roundel. These were in a Light Grey paint. The aircraft was later over-painted and finally allocated SAAF serial numbers. Note the pre-war style of roundel and that only the White section of the fin flash had been applied. The Blue portion of the Type A1 roundel on the fuselage has almost rubbed off completely with only two areas on the top and forward edge of it still visible. The serial number is applied in a small non-standard font in Black on the rear fuselage. The aircraft is heavily weathered and had fresh patches of paint applied, presumably where repair work was carried out. It also appears that the green areas on both the upper and lower wings have been over-painted in Dark Green.

Gloster Gladiator Mk. II, N2287/E, 3 Squadron. The same aircraft as above repainted in Dark Earth and Dark Green colours. The code letter E was retained but have been repositioned and standard roundels, but smaller than usual, have been applied. The code letter appears to be painted in White, but could possibly be in a Light Grey colour. The fin flash was also modified to consist of three vertical columns in Orange, White and Blue.

Curtiss Mohawk Mk. IV, 2511 (BS794). Mohawk 2511 was delivered to the SAAF in June 1941. The Mohawk served with 4 Squadron during their training period at 70 OTU, Nakuru, Kenya. It was a Presentation Aircraft and carried the name "Northern Transvaal" on the left hand side and "Noord Transvaal" (in Afrikaans) on the right hand side of the fuselage. The Northern Transvaal was a farming region stretching from north of Louis Trichard, across the Soutpansberg Mountain up to Messina on the northern border of the country. It was finished in the standard Temperate Land Scheme of Dark Green and Dark Earth upper surfaces, with RAF Sky lower surfaces. It carried standard roundels with Orange centres and fin flashes in Orange, White and Blue for the period. The serial numbers were painted in Black on the rear fuselage. The Mohawk survived the East African Campaign and on completion thereof, was flown to Zwartkops Air Station on 11 December 1941, for further service in the Union.

Curtiss Mohawk Mk. IV, 2524 (BJ550), 3 Squadron. Mohawk 2524 was delivered to the SAAF during March 1941. The aircraft served with 3 Squadron at Alomata during the East African Campaign, where 3 Squadron's A-Flight was based. When photographed at Alomata, it was finished in the standard Temperate Land Scheme of Dark Green and Dark Earth upper surfaces, with RAF Sky lower surfaces. It carried standard roundels with Orange centres and fin flashes in Orange, White and Blue for the period. The serial numbers were painted in Black on the rear fuselage and the 3 Squadron "Fighting Wasp" emblem was applied to the forward fuselage below the windshield. The emblem was a modified version of the original emblem that was applied to the Hawker Hurricanes. It is the authors' impression from the photograph that the emblem on this Mohawk was on a yellow background with all lettering and the wasp in stencil format in green paint. In the post-war era the emblem was also applied in this same fashion and colours on the Harvards operated by 3 Squadron. After the East African Campaign the Mohawk returned to the Union and was eventually issued to 6 Squadron.

Curtiss Mohawk Mk. IV, 2508 (BS787), 4 Squadron. Mohawk 2508 was delivered to the SAAF in June 1941. The Mohawk served with 4 Squadron during their training period at 70 OTU, Nakuru, Kenya. Thereafter it was transferred to 3 Squadron when they were equipped with Mohawks at Nanyuki, in August 1941. On 20 November 1941, the Mohawk was involved in further continuous air attacks ordered on positions in the Feroaber and Kulkaber Pass positions. During the operations Mohawk 2508 crashed on take-off from Alomata and the pilot, Lt G. R. Jacobs, was killed. It appeared that he had stalled the aircraft in a turn, did one and a half turns of a spin and dived into the ground. It was finished in the standard Temperate Land Scheme of Dark Green and Dark Earth upper surfaces, with RAF Sky lower surfaces. It carried standard roundels with Orange centres and fin flashes in Orange, White and Blue for the period. The serial numbers were painted in Black on the rear fuselage and when photographed at Nakuru, it had no unit emblem applied yet. A paint patch is visible on the rear fuselage where the original RAF serial number was painted out and replaced by the SAAF serial number.

Curtiss Mohawk Mk. IV, 2537 (BJ536), 3 Squadron. Mohawk 2537 was delivered to the SAAF during May 1941. The aircraft served with 3 Squadron at Alomata where it was photographed wearing the modified version of the 3 Squadron emblem. It also had a dark coloured wheel disk and propeller hub, presumably indicating the colours of one of the Flights. It has been illustrated in Red in the colour plate, illustrating an aircraft allocated to A-Flight. There is no further record of this aircraft in any of the War Diaries of the SAAF units that operated the Mohawk IVs. It was finished in the standard Temperate Land Scheme of Dark Green and Dark Earth upper surfaces, with RAF Sky lower surfaces. It carried standard roundels with Orange centres and fin flashes in Orange, White and Blue for the period. The serial numbers were painted in Black on the rear fuselage and the 3 Squadron "Fighting Wasp" emblem was applied to the forward fuselage below the windshield. It is the authors' impression from the photograph that the emblem on this Mohawk was on a light blue (possibly SAAF Sky Blue) background with all lettering and the wasp in stencil format in black paint.

Hurricane Mk. I, 277 (L1909), 2 Squadron, Mombasa, October 1941. Exterior finish consisted of Dark Green and Dark Earth upper surfaces, with SAAF Sky Blue lower surfaces. National insignia consisted of SAAF Type A fuselage roundels and SAAF Type A lower wing roundels, all with Orange centres. The upper wing roundels were modified Type A roundels in which the White was over-painted with Orange and Blue to form Type B roundels with a Yellow outer ring. These were later replaced with standard SAAF Type B roundels. The fin flashes were in Orange, White and Blue. Individual aircraft markings consisted of the serial number in Black on the rear fuselage and the code letter Q in a Light Grey paint on the rear fuselage. During its early service this aircraft carried the name "Goof" on both sides of the forward fuselage in what appears to be White paint. The over-painted lower surface serial numbers, L1909, were still slightly visible through the thin coat of SAAF Sky Blue applied to the lower wing surfaces. Hurricane 277 was delivered to the SAAF during September 1939. The aircraft departed for East Africa and was allocated to 1 Squadron on 22 May 1940. After initially serving with 1 Squadron it was transferred to 2 Squadron when the section of 1 Squadron in Nairobi, was renumbered, on 1 October 1940. The Hurricane was transferred to 3 Squadron on 1 December 1940, along with 272, to be used as reserve aircraft. Hurricane 277 was of the early Mk. I version, fitted with fabric covered wings and two-bladed propeller. Note that it also still had the earlier type of pitot tube and antenna mast fitted.

Next page Hurricane Mk. I, 279/D, 3 Squadron, January 1941. Exterior finish consisted of Dark Green and Dark Earth upper surfaces, with SAAF Sky Blue lower surfaces. National insignia consisted of SAAF Type A1 fuselage roundels, SAAF Type B upper wing roundels and SAAF Type A lower wing roundels, all with Orange centres. The fin flashes were in Orange, White and Blue. Unit insignia consisted of the 3 Squadron "Fighting Wasp" emblem applied to both sides of the nose. Individual aircraft markings consisted of the serial number in Black on the rear fuselage and the code letter D applied most likely in Orange to the rear fuselage. Hurricane 279 was flown by 2/Lt J. P. Upton from Waterkloof Air Station to Nairobi, when 3 Squadron originally deployed to East Africa. This Hurricane was destroyed in a crash on 3 June 1941, when Lt A. S. Venter crashed into a hillside in bad weather conditions.

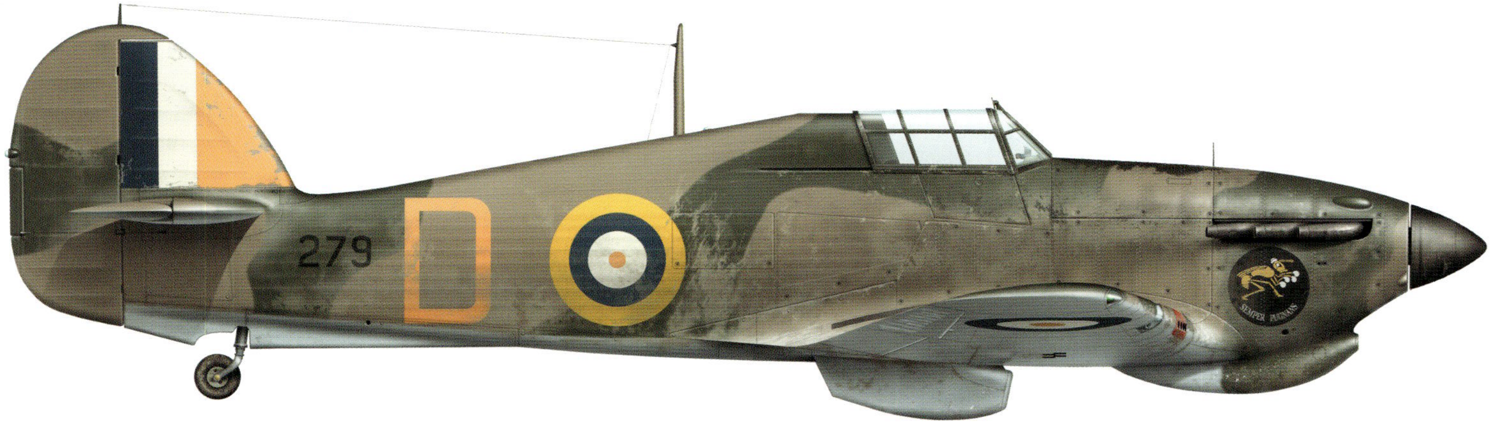

Below Hurricane Mk I, 284/J, 3 Squadron, Dagahbur, 15 March 1941. Exterior finish consisted of Dark Green and Dark Earth upper surfaces, with SAAF Sky Blue lower surfaces. National insignia consisted of SAAF Type A1 fuselage roundels, SAAF Type B upper wing roundels and SAAF Type A lower wing roundels, all with orange centres. The fin flashes were in Orange, White and Blue. Individual aircraft markings consisted of the serial number in Black on the rear fuselage and the individual code letter in Light Grey on the rear fuselage. Lt Robert H. C. "Bob" Kershaw piloted this Hurricane during the dramatic rescue of Capt Jack Frost on 15 March 1941. For this action he received an immediate award of the D.S.O. for his personal courage and determination. This was the first D.S.O. to be awarded to the SAAF during W.W. II. Lt Kershaw had seen the smoking aircraft of his flight commander land on the satellite airfield. With the Italian artillery shelling the aerodrome from the hills above, Lt. Kershaw decided to land and pick up Capt Frost. After landing he taxied over to the crashed Hurricane, undid his harness and shouted for his Flight Commander to jump in. After an agonising 45 minute flight, they safely landed back at their aerodrome in Dagahbur.

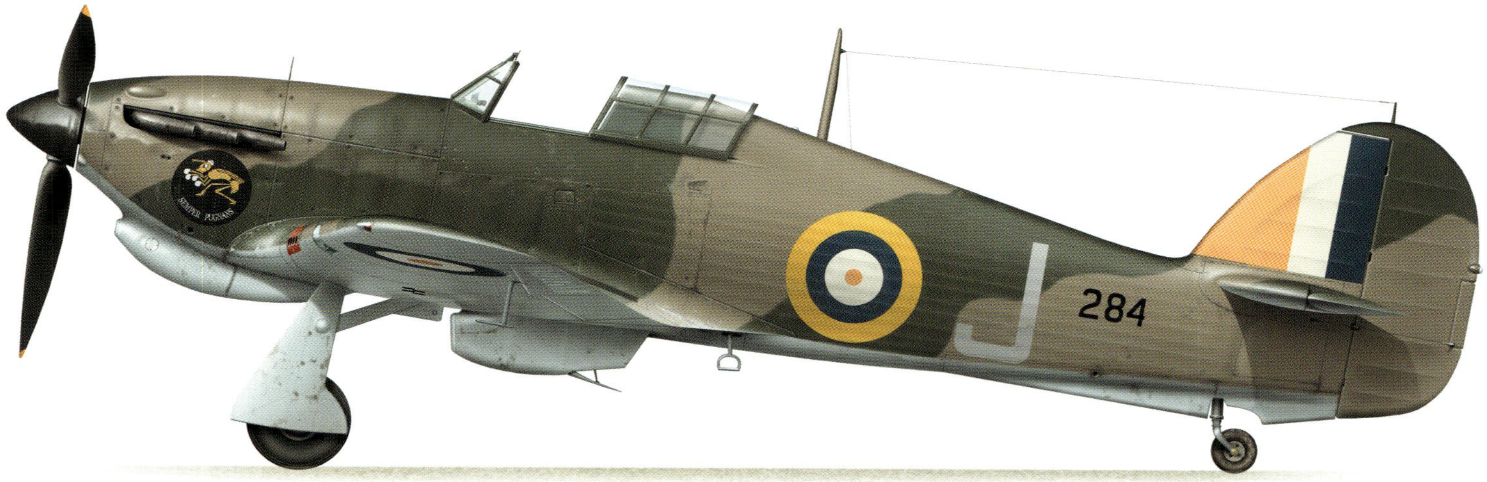

Hurricane Mk. I, 289 (P3253), 3 Squadron, Diredawa, April 1941. Exterior finish consisted of Dark Green and Dark Earth upper surfaces, with SAAF Sky Blue lower surfaces. National insignia consisted of SAAF Type A fuselage roundels, SAAF Type B upper wing roundels and SAAF Type A lower wing roundels, all with orange centres. The fin flashes were in Orange, White and Blue. The Unit marking on this aircraft consisted of the "Fighting Wasp" insignia of 3 Squadron, in modified colours, indicating Capt Jack Frost's Flight Commander status. Individual aircraft markings consisted of the serial number in Black on the rear fuselage and the individual code letter in Yellow on the rear fuselage. This was the personal Hurricane of Capt John Everitt "Jack" Frost D.F.C. and Bar from 25 March 1941, until the end of his 3 Squadron tour, on 19 May 1941. On 30 March he engaged 2 S.79s with Lt Howitson and both enemy bombers were damaged. On 5 April, he strafed aircraft on the ground at Addis Abeba and left 3 S.79s and a Ca.133 burning. In a follow-up attack later in the day, he left another S.79 and one more Ca.133s burning as well. During a strafing attack on Dessye on 6 April, he left two CR.42 fighters and two S.79 bombers burning, while he left two CR.42s burning on the ground at Sciasciamanna on 10 April. A second attack on this date led to a CR.42 shot down, with Lt Howitson, and a CR.32 and Caproni bomber burning on the airfield at Gimma. An attack on Gimma on 13 April, left a Ro.37 fighter and a Caproni burning, followed by another successful attack on Dessye on the 16th, leaving one CR.32 and two CR.42 fighters burning. Regular attacks were carried out on Gimma during the last few days of April and on 30 April he shot down another S.79 bomber, with five crew-members baling out, as well as leaving one CR.32 burning on the airfield at Gimma. During the first few days of May 1941 a number of vehicles were shot up by him during attacks on road convoys, until the taking of Addis Ababa.

Next page Hurricane Mk. IIB, HV490/X, 41 Squadron, East Africa 1942. The Hurricane was taken on strength in late October 1942. On arrival the aircraft was finished in the standard Temperate Land Colour Scheme of Dark Green and Dark Earth upper surfaces, with Sky lower surfaces. The aircraft had white distemper markings added to the rear fuselage and tailplanes for the ferry flight from Takoradi. It carried standard roundels for the period, namely Type C1 on the fuselage, Type C under wing and Type B upper wing, with the centres in Orange and the fin flash consisted of Orange, White and Blue bands. The individual code letter was applied in White paint, while the serial number was applied in Black to the rear fuselage. The spinner appears to be finished in Red on this particular aircraft. This aircraft was in the fourth flight to route from Gilgal to Mombasa in December 1942.

Below Hurricane Mk. IIB, HV500/Q, 41 Squadron, East Africa 1942. The Hurricane was taken on strength in October 1942. On arrival the aircraft was finished in the standard Temperate Land Colour Scheme of Dark Green and Dark Earth upper surfaces, with Sky lower surfaces. The aircraft had White distemper markings added to the rear fuselage and tailplanes for the ferry flight from Takoradi. It carried standard roundels for the period, namely Type C1 on the fuselage, Type C under wing and Type B upper wing, with the centres in Orange, and the fin flash consisted of Orange, White and Blue bands. The individual code letter was applied in White paint, while the serial number was applied in Black to the rear fuselage. The spinner appears to be finished in Red on this particular aircraft. It was damaged at Nanyuki on 12 November, when an Avro Anson which was taxiing in, collided with it. Fairly extensive damage was caused to the tail end and empennage. It was repaired, resulting in the non-standard camouflage and repaint of the rear fuselage and lower wing, removing the roundel. It was part of the 5th Flight when the aircraft were ferried to Mombasa during December 1942. This Hurricane took part in the operation in French Somailand during the last few days of December 1942.

Appendices

Appendix 1: Additional Gladiator colours

Top Gloster Gladiator Mk. I, K Flight, East Africa 1941. The SAAF did not operate Gladiator Mk. Is in their squadrons, but 1 Squadron operated with K Flight on a number of occasions during the attacks on Gallabat and in the Metama area, and this unit did fly Gladiator Mk. Is. 1 Squadron was tasked to fly escort missions with their Gladiator Mk. IIs for the K Flight Gladiator Mk. Is, while they were engaged in bombing operations.

Midlde Gloster Gladiator Mk. II, N22xx/GO, 3 Squadron, East Africa 1941. After losing a number of Hawker Hurricanes, 3 Squadron was reinforced with nine Gladiators from 94 Squadron RAF. The Gladiator in picture still carries the GO squadron identification code of 94 Squadron and the aircraft were only over-painted and allocated SAAF serial numbers at a later date. Note the tail flash with the narrow bands, the smaller roundels and the presumed Sky tail band of the aircraft, although the band on this specific aircraft might have been in White. The Gladiator is finished in four colours of the Temperate Land Scheme for biplanes, but is heavily weathered. The lower left surface area is finished in Black, while the right hand side lower surface is in White. The individual and unit code letters are in a light grey colour, while the serial numbers on these aircraft were in a small non-standard font in Black paint on the rear fuselages. The roundels still had the RAF Red centres when received. The fuselage carried Type A1 roundels, as well as the lower left hand wing, while the lower right hand wing carried a Type A roundel. The top surfaces of the upper wings had Type B roundels applied to them.

Bottom Gloster Gladiator Mk II, N22xx/GO, 3 Squadron, East Africa 1941. The Gladiator is finished in four colours of the Temperate Land Scheme for biplanes, but is heavily weathered. The lower left surface area is finished in Black, while the right hand side lower surfaces is in White. The individual and unit code letters appear to be in a light grey colour, while the serial numbers on these aircraft were in a small non-standard font in Black paint on the rear fuselages. The roundels still had the RAF Red centres when received. The Gladiator has a tail band around the rear fuselage, in what is believed to be standard RAF Sky, with heavy weathering on it and the lower colours showing through. Note the modified fin flash with the narrow bands and the replacement Aluminium canopy bars. The Yellow outer ring of the Type A1 roundel applied to the black-painted lower left hand wing is also clearly visible.

Top Gloster Gladiator Mk. II, N5813, from 1 Squadron, while refuelling at Kosti, on the White Nile, before continuing southwards to Nairobi, Kenya in July 1940. Kosti was a pre-war Imperial Airways Cairo – Cape Town stop on the White Nile River. The Gladiator is finished in four colours of the Temperate Land Scheme for biplanes, with Black and White lower surfaces, split down the fuselage centre line. National markings consisted of SAAF Type A1 fuselage roundels, a SAAF Type A1 roundel below the lower left wing, a SAAF Type A roundel below the lower right hand wing and Type B roundels on the upper surfaces of both top wings. The fin flashes were in Orange, White and Blue. Individual markings consisted of the serial number in Black on the rear fuselage. Note the larger size of the fuselage roundels. N5813 was shot down on 8 November 1940, by own anti-aircraft fire (Sudanese gunners) and over-turned during the crash-landing on an island in the Nile, 16 km south of Juba, while transferring from 2 Squadron to 1 Squadron.

Middle Gloster Gladiator Mk. II, N5818. The Gladiator was one of the first batch of nine aircraft to fly down to Nairobi on 24 July 1940 and was transferred to 2 Squadron, when that section of the original 1 Squadron was re-numbered. The aircraft was finished in the A-scheme camouflage pattern. The lower surfaces were finished in Aluminium, except for the bottom of the lower wings, which were finished in Black (left) and White (right). The lower left wing had a modified Type A1 roundel applied with a Yellow outer ring, to enhance the visibility of the Blue against the Black paint. On 13 October 1940, while serving with 2 Squadron, Lt. L. R. Dudley crashed the Gladiator in the lagoon just south of Port Reitz aerocdrome, during a low-level beat up. The pilot was safe and the Navy assisted with the salvage of the Gladiator. It was thereafter repaired by the SAAF. After the repair, the aircraft lower surfaces would have been finished in SAAF Sky Blue as per the standing orders from August 1940. The Gladiator was transferred back to the RAF during June 1941.

Bottom Gloster Gladiator Mk. II, 1333, 3 Squadron, 1941. The 3 Squadron Gladiators were eventually repainted and then received new serial numbers in the SAAF serial system and the block of 1321 to 1350 was allocated. This is Gladiator 1333 in the new simplified colour scheme of Dark Earth and Dark Green upper surfaces. The roundel is much smaller than previously. It appears from the tropical filter and the inside of the right hand landing gear that the lower surfaces have been re-painted in the SAAF Sky Blue colour, as per the orders issued in August 1940 already. A light area below the left wing suggests that Type A roundels have been applied below the bottom wing.

Appendix 2: Additional Hurricane colours

Top Hawker Hurricane Mk. I, L1710, 1 Squadron, Waterkloof Air Station, April 1940. Exterior finish on delivery from England consisted of Dark Green and Dark Earth upper surfaces, with Aluminium lower surfaces. National markings consisted of Type A fuselage roundels, Type A lower wing roundels and Type A1 upper wing roundels, all with Orange centres. No fin flashes were carried on delivery from England. Individual markings consisted of the serial number in Black on the rear fuselage and below both wings. This was the second of the first three Hurricanes received by the SAAF when these aircraft were delivered to Durban by sea during February 1939. The aircraft received the SAAF serial number 272 during April 1940.

Middle Hawker Hurricane Mk. I, 275 (ex-L1875), 3 Squadron, 1941. Exterior finish consisted of Dark Green and Dark Earth upper surfaces, with SAAF Sky Blue lower surfaces. National markings consisted of SAAF Type A1 roundels on the fuselage and SAAF Type A roundels on the lower wing surfaces, with SAAF Type B roundels on the upper wing surfaces. The fin flashes were in Orange, White and Blue. Squadron markings consisted of the "Fighting Wasp" insignia of 3 Squadron, applied to both sides of the nose during late November 1941, while individual aircraft markings were the serial numbers applied in Black on both rear fuselage sides. The Hurricane was delivered in South Africa in June 1939.

Bottom Hawker Hurricane Mk. I, 279/D, 3 Squadron, April 1941. Exterior finish consisted of Dark Green and Dark Earth upper surfaces, with SAAF Sky Blue lower surfaces. National insignia consisted of SAAF Type A1 fuselage roundels, SAAF Type B upper wing roundels and SAAF Type A lower wing roundels, all with Orange centres. The fin flashes were in Orange, White and Blue. Unit insignia consisted of the 3 Squadron "Fighting Wasp" emblem applied to both sides of the nose. Individual aircraft markings consisted of the serial number in Black on the rear fuselage and the code letter D applied in light grey to the rear fuselage. The sides of the tropical air filter have been camouflaged with what appear to be Dark Green paint, in order to reduce the visibility of the filter. This feature was noted on a number of later Hurricanes in the squadron. The Hurricane has clearly seen some heavy action, as can be seen by the patched appearance of the aircraft.